ABE LINCOLN
IN ILLINOIS

BY ROBERT EMMET SHERWOOD

ABE LINCOLN IN ILLINOIS

IDIOT'S DELIGHT

THE PETRIFIED FOREST

REUNION IN VIENNA

THIS IS NEW YORK

THE VIRTUOUS KNIGHT

WATERLOO BRIDGE

THE QUEEN'S HUSBAND

THE ROAD TO ROME

CHARLES SCRIBNER'S SONS

ABE LINCOLN IN ILLINOIS

A Play in Twelve Scenes

BY

ROBERT EMMET SHERWOOD

With a Foreword by Carl Sandburg

CHARLES SCRIBNER'S SONS · NEW YORK
CHARLES SCRIBNER'S SONS · LTD · LONDON
1939

Published, February, 1939

Second Printing, February, 1939
Third Printing, February, 1939

TO MY
MOTHER

ABE LINCOLN IN ILLINOIS

Presented by the Playwrights' Company—Maxwell Anderson, S. N. Behrman, Sidney Howard, Elmer Rice and Robert E. Sherwood—at the National Theatre, Washington, D. C., on October 3rd, and at the Plymouth Theatre, New York City, October 15th, 1938, with the following cast:

MENTOR GRAHAM	Frank Andrews
ABE LINCOLN	Raymond Massey
ANN RUTLEDGE	Adele Longmire
BEN MATTLING	George Christie
JUDGE BOWLING GREEN	Arthur Griffin
NINIAN EDWARDS	Lewis Martin
JOSHUA SPEED	Calvin Thomas
TRUM COGDAL	Harry Levian
JACK ARMSTRONG	Howard daSilva
BAB	Everett Charlton
FEARGUS	David Clarke
JASP	Kevin McCarthy
SETH GALE	Herbert Rudley
NANCY GREEN	Lillian Foster
WILLIAM HERNDON	Wendell K. Phillips
ELIZABETH EDWARDS	May Collins
MARY TODD	Muriel Kirkland
THE EDWARDS' MAID	Augusta Dabney
JIMMY GALE	Howard Sherman
AGGIE GALE	Marion Rooney
GOBEY	Hubert Brown
STEPHEN A. DOUGLAS	Albert Phillips
WILLIE LINCOLN	Lex Parrish
TAD LINCOLN	Lloyd Barry

ROBERT LINCOLN . . . . John Payne
THE LINCOLNS' MAID . . . . Iris Whitney
CRIMMIN . . . . Frank Tweddell
BARRICK . . . . John Gerard
STURVESON . . . . Thomas F. Tracey
JED . . . . Harry Levian
KAVANAGH . . . . Glenn Coulter
Major . . . . Everett Charlton

SOLDIERS, RAILROAD MEN, TOWNSPEOPLE

Allen Shaw, Phillip Caplan, Wardell Jennings, Dearon Darnay, Harrison Woodhull, Robert Fitzsimmons, Joseph Wiseman, Walter Kapp, Melvyn Dinellie, Bert Schorr, Ora Alexander, Richard Allen, Bette Benfield, Dorothy Greeley, David Hewes, Alfred Jenkins, George Malcolm, McKinley Reeves, Elizabeth Reller, Lotta Stawisky, Ann Stevenson.

Staged by Elmer Rice

Settings by Jo Mielziner

Stage Manager, Elmer Brown

Ass't. Stage Manager, John Triggs

CONTENTS

ix

FOREWORD
BY CARL SANDBURG

The Irish have a saying from the Gaelic about things so durable they will last "a thousand years and after that to the end of the world."

Of natural, personal, human legends the one of Lincoln will probably last as long as any known —and the end of the world is a long time.

For many years, probably many centuries, there are to be biographies about Lincoln—and dramas.

"Abe Lincoln in Illinois" by Robert E. Sherwood is the first full-statured drama that has come around the legend.

Also it is the first shaped by a playwright who went to the main studies derived from basic source materials—and delved extensively himself in the actual sources.

The extent to which he realized his responsibility—in availing himself of a dramatist's license to depart from the facts—is soberly told in his supplementary notes.

It may be that sometime we shall have a Lincoln drama employing entirely speeches and situations authenticated by documents and evidence—but whether it will be a drama that people will go to see and value as drama is another question.

Having seen Sherwood's play, and having noticed how the audience itself participated, I believe it carries some shine of the American dream, that it delivers great themes of human wit, behavior and freedom, with Lincoln as mouthpiece and instrument.

Also there are moments when the lines of Sherwood as rendered by Massey achieve an involved, baffling Hamlet of democracy. Or again there are twilights of motive as curious as a Chekhov short story. And one goes away from seeing the play haunted by some reality persuasive of Lincoln's presence, of his sobriety and wit, of his somber broodings over the Family of Man on the earth and the strange prices of devotion and discipline paid for the getting and keeping of freedom.

ACT I

ABE LINCOLN IN ILLINOIS

ACT I

SCENE I

MENTOR GRAHAM'S *cabin near New Salem, Illinois. Late at night.*

There is one rude table, piled with books and papers. Over it hangs an oil lamp, the only source of light.

At one side of the table sits MENTOR GRAHAM, *a sharp but patient schoolteacher.*

Across from him is ABE LINCOLN—*young, gaunt, tired but intent, dressed in the ragged clothes of a backwoodsman. He speaks with the drawl of southern Indiana—an accent which is more Kentuckian than middle-western.*

MENTOR *is leaning on the table.* ABE'S *chair is tilted back, so that his face is out of the light.* MENTOR *turns a page in a grammar book.*

MENTOR

The Moods. (MENTOR *closes the book and looks at* ABE.) Every one of us has many moods. You yourself have more than your share of them, Abe. They express the various aspects of your character. So it is with the English language—and you must try to consider this language as if it were a living person, who may be awkward and stumbling, or pompous and pretentious, or simple and direct. Name me the five moods.

ABE

The Indicative, Imperative, Potential, Subjunctive and Infinitive.

MENTOR

And what do they signify?

ABE

The Indicative Mood is the easy one. It just indicates a thing—like "He loves," "He is loved"—or, when you put it in the form of a question, "Does he love?" or "Is he loved?" The Imperative Mood is used for commanding, like "Get out and be damned to you."

MENTOR (*smiling*)

Is that the best example you can think of?

ABE

Well—you can put it in the Bible way—"Go thou in peace." But it's still imperative.

MENTOR

The mood derives its name from the implication of command. But you can use it in a very different sense—in the form of the humblest supplication.

Abe

Like "Give us this day our daily bread and forgive us our trespasses."

Mentor (*reaching for a newspaper in the mess on the table*)

I want you to read this—it's a speech delivered by Mr. Webster before the United States Senate. A fine document, and a perfect usage of the Imperative Mood in its hortatory sense. Here it is. Read this—down here. (*He leans back to listen.*)

Abe (*takes paper, leans forward into the light and reads*)

"Sir," the Senator continued, in the rich deep tones of the historic church bells of his native Boston, "Sir—I have not allowed myself to look beyond the Union, to see what might be hidden in the dark recess behind. While the Union lasts . . ." (*Abe has been reading in a monotone, without inflection.*)

Mentor (*testily*)

Don't read it off as if it were an inventory of Denton Offut's groceries. Imagine that *you're* making the speech before the Senate, with the fate of your country at stake. Put your own life into it!

Abe

I couldn't use words as long as Dan'l Webster.

Mentor

That's what you're here for—to learn! Go ahead.

ABE (*reading slowly, gravely*)

"While the Union lasts, we have high prospects spread out before us, for us and our children. Beyond that, I seek not to penetrate the veil. God grant that in my day, at least, the curtain may not rise."

MENTOR

Notice the use of verbs from here on.

ABE (*reads*)

"When my eyes shall be turned to behold for the last time the sun in heaven, may I not see him shining on the broken and dishonored fragments of a once glorious Union; on States dissevered, discordant, belligerent; on a land rent with civil feuds, or drenched, it may be, in fraternal blood! Let their last feeble glance rather behold the glorious ensign of the republic, now known and honored throughout the earth, not a single star of it obscured, bearing for its motto no such miserable interrogatory . . ." (*He stumbles over the pronunciation.*)

MENTOR

Interrogatory.

ABE (*continuing*)

". . . interrogatory as 'What is all this worth?' Nor, those other words of delusion and folly, 'Liberty first and Union afterwards'; but everywhere, spread all over in characters of living light, that other sentiment, dear to every true American heart—Liberty and Union . . ."

Mentor

Emphasize the "*and.*"

Abe

"Liberty *and* Union, now and forever, one and inseparable!" (*He puts the paper back on the table.*) He must have had 'em up on their feet cheering with *that*, all right.

Mentor

Some cheered, and some spat, depending on which section they came from.

Abe

What was he talking about?

Mentor

It was in the debate·over the right of any state to secede from the Union. Hayne had pleaded South Carolina's cause—pleaded it ably. He said that just as we have liberty as individuals—so have we liberty as states—to go as we please. Which means, if we don't like the Union, as expressed by the will of its majority, then we can leave it, and set up a new nation, or many nations —so that this continent might be as divided as Europe. But Webster answered him, all right. He proved that without Union, we'd have precious lit-

tle liberty left. Now—go on with the Potential
Mood.

ABE

That signifies possibility—usually of an unpleas-
ant nature. Like, "If I ever get out of debt, I will
probably get right back in again."

MENTOR (*smiles*)

Why did you select that example, Abe?

ABE

Well—it just happens to be the thought that's
always heaviest on my mind.

MENTOR

Is the store in trouble again?

ABE (*calmly*)

Yes. Berry's drunk all the whiskey we ought to
have sold, and we're going to have to shut up any
day now. I guess I'm my father's own son. Give
me a steady job, and I'll fail at it.

MENTOR

You haven't been a failure here, Abe. There
isn't a manjack in this community that isn't fond
of you and anxious to help you get ahead.

ABE (*with some bitterness*)

I know—just like you, Mentor, sitting up late
nights, to give me learning, out of the goodness of
your heart. And now, Josh Speed and Judge Green
and some of the others I owe money to want to

get me the job of post-master, thinking that maybe
I can handle *that*, since there's only one mail comes
in a week. I've got friends, all right—the best
friends. But they can't change my luck, or maybe
it's just my nature.

MENTOR

What you 'want to do is get out of New Salem.
This poor little forgotten town will never give
any one any opportunity.

ABE

Yes—I've thought about moving, think about it
all the time. My family have always been movers,
shifting about, never knowing what they were
looking for, and whatever it was, never finding it.
My old father ambled from Virginia, to one place
after another in Kentucky, where I was born, and
then into Indiana, and then here in Illinois. About
all I can remember of when I was a boy was hitching up, and then unhitching, and then hitching up
again.

MENTOR

Then get up and go, Abe. Make a new place
for yourself in a new world.

ABE

As a matter of fact, Seth Gale and me have been
talking a lot about moving—out to Kansas or
Nebraska territory. But—wherever I go—it'll be
the same story—more friends, more debts.

MENTOR

Well, Abe—just bear in mind that there are always two professions open to people who fail at everything else: there's school-teaching, and there's politics.

ABE

Then I'll choose school-teaching. You go into politics, and you may get elected.

MENTOR

Yes—there's always that possibility.

ABE

And if you get elected, you've got to go to the city. I don't want none of that.

MENTOR

What did I say about two negatives?

ABE

I meant, any of that.

MENTOR

What's your objection to cities, Abe? Have you ever seen one?

ABE

Sure. I've been down river twice to New Orleans. And, do you know, every minute of the time I was there, I was scared?

MENTOR

Scared of what, Abe?

ABE

Well—it sounds kind of foolish—I was scared of people.

MENTOR (*laughs*)

Did you imagine they'd rob you of all your gold and jewels?

ABE (*serious*)

No. I was scared they'd kill me.

MENTOR (*also serious*)

Why? Why should they want to kill you?

ABE

I don't know.

MENTOR (*after a moment*)

You think a lot about death, don't you?

ABE

I've had to, because it has always seemed to be so close to me—always—as far back as I can remember. When I was no higher than this table, we buried my mother. The milksick got her, poor creature. I helped Paw make the coffin—whittled the pegs for it with my own jackknife. We buried her in a timber clearing beside my grandmother, old Betsy Sparrow. I used to go there often and look at the place—used to watch the deer running over her grave with their little feet. I never could kill a deer after that. One time I catched hell from Paw because when he was taking aim I knocked his gun up. And I always compare the looks of those deer

with the looks of men—like the men in New Orleans—that you could see had murder in their
hearts.

MENTOR (*after a moment*)

You're a hopeless mess of inconsistency, Abe
Lincoln.

ABE

How do you mean, Mentor?

MENTOR

I've never seen any one who is so friendly and at
the same time so misanthropic.

ABE

What's that?

MENTOR

A misanthrope is one who distrusts men and
avoids their society.

ABE

Well—maybe that's how I am. Oh—I like people, well enough—when you consider 'em one by
one. But they seem to look different when they're
put into crowds, or mobs, or armies. But I came
here to listen to you, and then I do all the talking.

MENTOR

Go right on, Abe. I'll correct you when you
say things like "catched hell."

ABE (*grins*)

I know. Whenever I get talking about Paw, I

sort of fall back into his language. But—you've got your own school to teach tomorrow. I'll get along. (*He stands up.*)

MENTOR

Wait a minute. . . . (*He is fishing about among the papers. He takes out a copy of an English magazine.*) There's just one more thing I want to show you. It's a poem. (*He finds the place in the magazine.*) Here it is. You read it, Abe. (*He hands* ABE *the magazine.*)

(ABE *seats himself on the edge of the table, and holds the magazine under the light.*)

ABE (*reads*)

" 'On Death,' written at the age of nineteen by the late John Keats:

'Can death be sleep, when life is but a dream,
And scenes of bliss pass as a phantom by?
The transient (*he hesitates on that word*) pleas-
    ures as a vision seem,
And yet we think the greatest pain's to die. (*He
    moves closer to the light.*)
How strange it is that man on earth should roam,
And lead a life of woe, but not forsake
His rugged path—nor dare he view alone
His future doom—which is but to awake.' "
(*He looks at* MENTOR.) That sure is good, Mentor. It's *fine!* (*He is reading it again, to himself, when the lights fade.*)

END OF SCENE I

SCENE II

The Rutledge Tavern, New Salem. Noon on the Fourth of July.

It is a large room, with log walls, but with curtains on the windows and pictures on the walls to give it an air of dressiness. The pictures include likenesses of all the presidents from Washington to Jackson, and there is also a picture (evidently used for campaign purposes) of Henry Clay.

At the left is a door leading to the kitchen. At the back, toward the right, is the main entrance, which is open. The sun is shining brightly.

The furniture of the room consists of two tables, two benches, and various chairs and stools.

BEN MATTLING is seated on a bench at the rear of the room. He is an ancient, paunchy, watery-eyed veteran of the Revolution, and he wears a cocked hat and the tattered but absurd semblance of a Colonial uniform. JUDGE BOWLING GREEN and NINIAN EDWARDS come in, followed by JOSHUA SPEED. BOWLING is elderly, fat, gentle. NINIAN is young, tall, handsome, prosperous. JOSH is quiet, mild, solid, thoughtful, well-dressed

BOWLING (*as they come in*)

This is the Rutledge Tavern, Mr. Edwards. It's not precisely a gilded palace of refreshment.

14

NINIAN

Make no apologies, Judge Green. As long as the whiskey is wet.

(JOSH *has crossed to the door at the left. He calls off.*)

JOSH

Miss Rutledge.

ANN (*appearing at the door*)

Yes, Mr. Speed?

JOSH

Have you seen Abe Lincoln?

ANN

No. He's probably down at the foot races. (*She goes back into the kitchen. JOSH turns to* BOWLING.)

JOSH

I'll find Abe and bring him here.

NINIAN

Remember, Josh, we've got to be back in Springfield before sundown.

(JOSH *has gone out.*)

BOWLING (*to* MATTLING)

Ah, good day, Uncle Ben. Have a seat, Mr. Edwards.

(*They cross to the table at the right.*)

BEN

Good day to you, Bowling.

(ANN *comes in from the kitchen.*)

ANN

Hello, Judge Green.

BOWLING

Good morning, Ann. We'd be grateful for a bottle of your father's best whiskey.

ANN

Yes, Judge. (*She starts to go off.*)

BEN (*stopping her*)

And git me another mug of that Barbadoes rum.

ANN

I'm sorry, Mr. Mattling, but I've given you one already and you know my father said you weren't to have any more till you paid for . . .

BEN

Yes, wench—I know what your father said. But if a veteran of the Revolutionary War is to be denied so much as credit, then this country has forgot its gratitude to them that made it.

BOWLING

Bring him the rum, Ann. I'll be happy to pay for it.

(TRUM COGDAL *comes in. He is elderly, persnicketty.*)

BEN (*reluctantly*)

I have to say thank you, Judge.

TRUM

Ann, bring me a pot of Sebago tea.

ANN

Yes, Mr. Cogdal. (*She goes out at the left.*
TRUM *sits down at the table.*)

BOWLING

Don't say a word, Ben.

TRUM

Well, Mr. Edwards—what's your impression of
our great and enterprising metropolis?

NINIAN

Distinctly favorable, Mr. Cogdal. I could not
fail to be impressed by the beauty of your location,
here on this hilltop, in the midst of the prairie land.

TRUM

Well, we're on the highroad to the West—and
when we get the rag, tag and bobtail cleaned out
of here, we'll grow. Yes, sir—we'll grow!

NINIAN (*politely*)

I'm sure of it.

(ANN *has returned with the whiskey, rum and
tea.*)

BOWLING

Thank you, Ann.

ANN

Has the mud-wagon come in yet?

TRUM

No. I been waiting for it.

BOWLING

Not by any chance expecting a letter, are you, Ann?

ANN

Oh, no—who'd be writing to *me*, I'd like to know?

BOWLING

Well—you never can tell what might happen on the Fourth of July. (*He and* NINIAN *lift their glasses.*) But I beg to wish you all happiness, my dear. And let me tell you that Mr. Edwards here is a married man, so you can keep those lively eyes to yourself.

ANN (*giggles*)

Oh, Judge Green—you're just joking me! (*She goes to the kitchen.*)

NINIAN

A mighty pretty girl.

TRUM

Comes of good stock, too.

NINIAN

With the scarcity of females in these parts, it's a wonder some one hasn't snapped her up.

BOWLING

Some one has. The poor girl promised herself to a man who called himself McNiel—it turned out his real name's McNamar. Made some money out here and then left town, saying he'd return soon. She's still waiting for him. But your time is short, Mr. Edwards, so if you tell us just what it is you want in New Salem, we'll do our utmost to . . .

NINIAN

I'm sure you gentlemen know what I want.

TRUM

Naturally, you want votes. Well—you've got mine. Anything to frustrate that tyrant, Andy Jackson. (*He shakes a finger at the picture of* ANDREW JACKSON.)

NINIAN

I assure you that I yield to none in my admiration for the character of our venerable president, but when he goes to the extent of ruining our banking structure, destroying faith in our currency and even driving sovereign states to the point of secession, then, gentlemen, it is time to call a halt.

BOWLING

We got two more years of him—if the old man lives that long. You can't make headway against his popularity.

NINIAN

But we can start now to drive out his minions here in the government of the state of Illinois. We have a great battle cry, "End the reign of Andrew Jackson."

(JACK ARMSTRONG and three others of the *Clary's Grove boys have come in during this speech. The others are named* BAB, FEARGUS *and* JASP. *They are the town bullies—boisterous, good-natured but tough.*)

JACK (*going to the door at the left*)
Miss Rutledge!

ANN (*appearing in the doorway*)
What do *you* want, Jack Armstrong?

JACK
Your humble pardon, Miss Rutledge, and we will trouble you for a keg of liquor.

BAB
And we'll be glad to have it quick, because we're powerful dry.

ANN
You get out of here—you get out of here right now—you low *scum!*

JACK
I believe I said a keg of liquor. Did you hear me say it, boys?

FEARGUS
That's how it sounded to me, Jack.

JASP
Come along with it, Annie——

Ann

If my father were here, he'd take a gun to you, just as he would to a pack of prairie wolves.

Jack

If your Paw was here, he'd be scareder than you. 'Cause he knows we're the wildcats of Clary's Grove, worse'n any old wolves, and we're a-howlin', and a-spittin' for drink. So get the whiskey, Miss Annie, and save your poor old Paw a lot of expenses for damages to his property.

(Ann *goes.*)

Trum (*in an undertone to* Ninian)

That's the rag, tag and bobtail I was . . .

Jack

And what are you mumblin' about, old measely-weasely Trum Cogdal—with your cup of tea on the Fourth of July?

Bab

He's a cotton-mouthed traitor and I think we'd better whip him for it.

Feargus (*at the same time*)

Squeeze that air tea outen him, Jack.

Jasp (*shouting*)

Come on you, Annie, with that liquor!

Jack

And you, too, old fat-pot Judge Bowling Green

that sends honest men to prison—and who's the stranger? Looks kind of damn elegant for New Salem.

BOWLING

This is Mr. Ninian Edwards of Springfield, Jack —and for the Lord's sake, shut up, and sit down, and behave yourselves.

JACK

Ninian Edwards, eh! The Governor's son, I presume. Well—well!

NINIAN (*amiably*)

You've placed me.

JACK

No wonder you've got a New Orleans suit of clothes and a gold fob and a silver-headed cane. I reckon you can buy the best of everything with that steamin' old pirate land-grabber for a Paw. I guess them fancy pockets of yourn are pretty well stuffed with the money your Paw stole from us tax-payers—eh, Mr. Edwards?

BAB

Let's take it offen him, Jack.

FEARGUS

Let's give him a lickin', Jack.

JACK (*still to* NINIAN)

What you come here for anyway? Lookin' for

a fight? Because if that's what you're a-cravin',
I'm your man—wrasslin', clawin', bitin', and tearin'.

ANN (*coming in*)

Jack Armstrong, here's your liquor! Drink it
and go away.

(ANN *carries four mugs.*)

JASP

He told you to bring a keg!

JACK (*contemplating the mugs*)

One little noggin apiece? Why—that ain't enough
to fill a hollow tooth! Get the keg, Annie.

FEARGUS

Perhaps she can't tote it. I'll get it, Jack. (*He
goes out into the kitchen.*)

ANN (*desperate*)

Aren't there any of you men can do anything to
protect decent people from these ruffians?

NINIAN

I'll be glad to do whatever I . . . (*He starts to
rise.*)

BOWLING (*restraining him*)

I'd be rather careful, Mr. Edwards.

JACK

That's right, Mr. Edwards. You be careful.
Listen to the old Squire. He's got a round pot but
a level head. He's seen the Clary's Grove boys in

action, and he can tell you you might get that silver-headed cane rammed down your gullet. Hey, Bab—you tell him what we did to Hank Spears and Gus Hocheimer. Just tell him!

BAB

Jack nailed the two of 'em up in a barr'l and sent 'em rollin' down Salem hill and it jumped the bank and fotched up in the river and when we opened up the barr'l they wasn't inclined to move much.

JACK

Of course, it'd take a bigger barr'l to hold you and your friend here, Squire, but I'd do it for you and I'd do it for any by God rapscallions and sons of thieves that come here a-preachin' treachery and disunion and pisenin' the name of Old Hickory, the people's friend.

(FEARGUS *returns with the keg.*)

BEN

Kill him, boys! You're the only *real* Americans we got left!

NINIAN (*rising*)

If you gentlemen will step outside, I'll be glad to accommodate you with the fight you seem to be spoiling for.

TRUM

You're committing suicide, Mr. Edwards.

JACK

Oh, no—he ain't. We ain't killers—we're just bone

crushers. After a few months, you'll be as good as new, which ain't saying much. You bring that keg, Feargus.

(*They are about to go when* ABE *appears in the door. He now is slightly more respectably dressed, wearing a battered claw-hammer coat and pants that have been "foxed" with buckskin. He carries the mail. Behind him is* JOSH SPEED.)

ABE

The mud-wagon's in! Hello, Jack. Hello, boys. Ain't you fellers drunk yet? Hello, Miss Ann. Got a letter for you. (*There is a marked shyness in his attitude toward* ANN.)

ANN

Thank you, Abe. (*She snatches the letter and runs out with it.*)

BEN

Abe, there's goin' to be a fight!

NINIAN (*to* JACK)

Well—come on, if you're coming.

JACK

All right, boys.

ABE

Fight? Who—and why?

JACK

This is the son of Ninian Edwards, Abe. Come

from Springfield lookin' for a little crotch hoist
and I'm aimin' to oblige.

(ABE *looks* NINIAN *over.*)

BOWLING

Put a stop to it, Abe. It'd be next door to murder.

JACK

You shut your trap, Pot Green. Murder's too
good for any goose-livered enemy of Andy Jackson.
Come on, boys!

ABE

Wait a minute, boys. Jack, have you forgotten
what day it is?

JACK

No, I ain't! But I reckon the Fourth is as good
a day as any to whip a politician!

ABE (*amiably*)

Well, if you've just got to fight, Jack, you
shouldn't give preference to strangers. Being postmaster of this thriving town, I can rate as a politician, myself, so you'd better try a fall with me—
(*He thrusts* JACK *aside and turns to* NINIAN.) And
as for you, sir, I haven't the pleasure of your acquaintance; but my name's Lincoln, and I'd like to
shake hands with a brave man.

NINIAN (*shaking hands with* ABE)

I'm greatly pleased to know you, Mr. Lincoln.

ABE

You should be. Because I come here just in time to save you quite some embarrassment, not to mention injury. Oh, got a couple of letters for you, Bowling. And here's your *Cincinnati Journal*, Trum.

JACK

Look here, Abe—you're steppin' into something that ain't none of your business. This is a private matter of patriotic honor . . .

ABE

Everything in this town is my business, Jack. It's the only kind of business I've got. And besides —I saw Hannah down by the grove and she says to tell you to come on to the picnic and that means *now* or she'll give the cake away to the Straders children and you and the boys'll go hungry. So get moving.

FEARGUS (*to* JACK)

Are you goin' to let Abe talk you out of it?

ABE

Sure he is. (*He turns to* TRUM.) Say, Trum— if you ain't using that *Journal* for a while, would you let me have a read?

TRUM

By all means, Abe. Here you are. (*He tosses the paper to* ABE.)

ABE

Thanks. (*He turns again to* JACK.) You'd better hurry, Jack, or *you'll* get a beating from Hannah.

(*He starts to take the wrapper off, as he goes over to a chair at the left.* JACK *looks at* ABE *for a moment, then laughs.*)

JACK (*to* NINIAN)

All right! Abe Lincoln's saved your hide. I'll consent to callin' off the fight just because he's a friend of mine.

ABE (*as he sits*)

And also because I'm the only one around here you can't lick.

JACK

But I just want to tell you, Mr. Ninian Edwards, Junior, that the next time you come around here a-spreadin' pisen and . . .

ABE

Go on, Jack. Hannah's waiting.

JACK (*walking over to* ABE)

I'm going, Abe. But I warn you—you'd better stop this foolishness of readin'—readin'—readin', mornin', noon and night, or you'll be gettin' soft and you won't be the same fightin' man you are now—and it would break my heart to see you licked by anybody, includin' me! (*He laughs, slaps* ABE *on the back, then turns to go.*) Glad to have met you, Mr. Edwards.

(*He goes out, followed by* BAB *and* JASP. FEAR-GUS *picks up the keg and starts after them.*)

NINIAN (*to* JACK)

It's been a pleasure.

ABE

Where'd you get that keg, Feargus?

FEARGUS (*nervously*)

Jack told me to take it outen Mis' Rutledge's kitchen and I . . .

ABE

Well—put it down. . . . If you see Seth Gale, tell him I've got a letter for him.

FEARGUS

I'll tell him, Abe.

(FEARGUS *puts down the keg and goes.* JOSH SPEED *laughs and comes up to the table.*)

JOSH

Congratulations, Ninian. I shouldn't have enjoyed taking you home to Mrs. Edwards after those boys had done with you.

NINIAN (*grinning*)

I was aware of the certain consequences, Josh. (*He turns to* ABE.) I'm deeply in your debt, Mr. Lincoln.

ABE

Never mind any thanks, Mr. Edwards. Jack Armstrong talks big but he means well.

Ninian

Won't you join us in a drink?

Abe

No, thank you.

(*He's reading the paper.* Bowling *fills the glasses.*)

Bowling

I'm going to have another! I don't mind telling you, I'm still trembling. (*He hands a glass to* Ninian, *then drinks himself.*)

Trum

You see, Mr. Edwards. It's that very kind of lawlessness that's holding our town back.

Ninian

You'll find the same element in the capital of our nation, and everywhere else, these days. (*He sits down and drinks.*)

Abe

Say, Bowling! It says here that there was a riot in Lyons, France. (*He reads.*) "A mob of men, deprived of employment when textile factories installed the new sewing machines, re-enacted scenes of the Reign of Terror in the streets of this prosperous industrial center. The mobs were suppressed only when the military forces of His French Majesty took a firm hand. The rioters carried banners inscribed with the incendiary words,

'We will live working or die fighting!' " (ABE *looks at the group at the right.*) That's Revolution!

BOWLING

Maybe, but it's a long way off from New Salem.

JOSH

Put the paper down, Abe. We want to talk to you.

ABE

Me? What about? (*He looks curiously at* JOSH, BOWLING *and* NINIAN.)

JOSH

I brought Mr. Edwards here for the sole purpose of meeting you—and with his permission, I shall tell you why.

NINIAN

Go right ahead, Josh.
(*All are looking intently at* ABE.)

JOSH

Abe—how would you like to run for the State Assembly?

ABE

When?

JOSH

Now—for the election in the fall.

ABE

Why?

NINIAN

Mr. Lincoln, I've known you for only a few minutes, but that's long enough to make me agree with Josh Speed that you're precisely the type of man we want. The whole Whig organization will support your candidacy.

ABE

This was all your idea, Josh?

JOSH (*smiling*)

Oh, no, Abe—you're the people's choice!

TRUM

What do *you* think of it, Bowling?

BOWLING (*heartily*)

I think it's as fine a notion as I ever heard. Why, Abe—I can hear you making speeches, right and left, taking your stand on all the issues—secession, Texas, the National Bank crisis, abolitionism—it'll be more fun than we ever had in our lives!

ABE (*rising*)

Isn't anybody going to ask what *I* think?

JOSH (*laughs*)

All right, Abe—*I'll* ask you.

ABE (*after a moment's pause*)

It's a comical notion, all right—and I don't know if I can give you an answer to it, offhand. But my first, hasty impression is that I don't think much of it.

BOWLING

Don't overlook the fact that, if elected, your salary would be three whole dollars a day.

ABE

That's fine money. No doubt of that. And I see what you have in mind, Bowling. I owe you a considerable sum of money; and if I stayed in the legislature for, say, twenty years, I'd be able to pay off—let me see—two dollars and a half a day. ... (*He is figuring it up on his fingers.*)

BOWLING

I'm not thinking about the debts, Abe.

ABE

I know you ain't, Bowling. But I've got to. And so should you, Mr. Edwards. The Whig party is the party of sound money and God save the National Bank, ain't it?

NINIAN

Why, yes—among other things. . . .

ABE

Well, then—how would it look if you put forward a candidate who has demonstrated no earning power but who has run up the impressive total of fifteen hundred dollars of debts?

BOWLING (*to* NINIAN)

I can tell you something about those debts. Abe started a grocery store in partnership with an unfortunate young man named Berry. Their stock included whiskey, and Berry started tapping the keg until he had consumed all the liquid assets. So the store went bankrupt—and Abe voluntarily assumed all the obligations. That may help to explain to you, Mr. Edwards, why we think pretty highly of him around here.

NINIAN

It's a sentiment with which I concur most heartily.

ABE

I thank you one and all for your kind tributes, but don't overdo them, or I'll begin to think that three dollars a day ain't enough!

JOSH

What's the one thing that you want most, Abe? You want to learn. This will give you your chance to get at a good library, to associate with the finest lawyers in the State.

ABE

I've got a copy of Blackstone, already. Found it in an old junk barrel. And how can I tell that the finest lawyers would welcome association with *me?*

NINIAN

You needn't worry about that. I saw how you dealt with those ruffians. You quite obviously know how to handle men.

ABE

I can handle the Clary's Grove boys because I can outwrassle them—but I can't go around Sangamon County throwing *all* the voters.

BOWLING (*laughing*)

I'll take a chance on that, Abe.

ABE (*to* NINIAN)

Besides—how do you know that my political views would agree with yours? How do you know I wouldn't say the wrong thing?

NINIAN

What *are* your political leanings, Mr. Lincoln?

ABE

They're all toward staying out. . . . What sort of leanings did you want?

NINIAN

We have a need for good conservative men to counteract all the radical firebrands that have swept over this country in the wake of Andrew Jackson. We've got to get this country back to first principles!

ABE

Well—I'm conservative, all right. If I got into

the legislature you'd never catch me starting any
movements for reform or progress. I'm pretty certain I wouldn't even have the nerve to open my
mouth.

JOSH (*laughs*)

I told you, Ninian—he's just the type of candidate you're looking for.

(NINIAN *laughs too, and rises.*)

NINIAN (*crossing towards* ABE)

The fact is, Mr. Lincoln, we want to spike the
rumor that ours is the party of the more privileged
classes. That is why we seek men of the plain people for candidates. As postmaster, you're in an excellent position to establish contacts. While de-
livering letters, you can also deliver speeches and
campaign literature, with which our headquarters
will keep you supplied.

ABE

Would you supply me with a suit of store
clothes? A candidate mustn't look *too* plain.

NINIAN (*smiling*)

I think even that could be arranged, eh, Judge?

BOWLING

I think so.

NINIAN (*pompously*)

So—think it over, Mr. Lincoln, and realize that
this is opportunity unlimited in scope. Just consider what it means to be starting up the ladder in

a nation which is now expanding southward, across the vast area of Texas; and westward, to the Empire of the Californias on the Pacific Ocean. We're becoming a continent, Mr. Lincoln—and all that we need is men! (*He looks at his watch.*) And now, gentlemen, if you will excuse me—I must put in an appearance at the torch-light procession in Springfield this evening, so I shall have to be moving on. Good-bye, Mr. Lincoln. This meeting has been a happy one for me.

ABE (*shaking hands*)

Good-bye, Mr. Edwards. Good luck in the campaign.

NINIAN

And the same to you.

(*All at the right have risen and are starting to go, except* BEN MATTLING, *who is still sitting at the back, drinking.*)

ABE

Here's your paper, Trum.

TRUM

Go ahead and finish it, Abe. I won't be looking at it yet awhile.

ABE

Thanks, Trum. I'll leave it at your house.

(TRUM *and* NINIAN *have gone.*)

BOWLING

I'll see you later, Abe. Tell Ann I'll be back to pay for the liquor.

ABE

I'll tell her, Bowling.

(BOWLING *goes.* JOSH *is looking at* ABE, *who, after a moment, turns to him.*)

ABE

I'm surprised at you, Josh. I thought you were my friend.

JOSH

I know, Abe. But Ninian Edwards asked me is there anybody in that God-forsaken town of New Salem that stands a chance of getting votes, and the only one I could think of was you. I can see you're embarrassed by this—and you're annoyed. But—whether you like it or not—you've got to grow; and here's your chance to get a little scrap of importance.

ABE

Am I the kind that wants importance?

JOSH

You'll deny it, Abe—but you've got a funny kind of vanity—which is the same as saying you've got some pride—and it's badly in need of nourishment. So, if you'll agree to this—I don't think you'll be sorry for it or feel that I've betrayed you.

ABE (*grins*)

Oh—I won't hold it against you, Josh. (*He walks away and looks out the door.*) But that Mr. Ninian Edwards—he's rich and he's prominent and

he's got a high-class education. Politics to him
is just a kind of a game. And maybe I'd like it
if I could play it *his* way. (*He turns to* Josh.)
But when you get to reading Blackstone, not to
mention the Bible, you can't help feeling maybe
there's some serious responsibility in the giving
of laws—and maybe there's something more important in the business of government than just getting the Whig Party back into power.

(Seth Gale *comes in. He is a young, husky
frontiersman, with flashes of the sun of Western
empire in his eyes.*)

Seth

Hey, Abe—Feargus said you've got a letter for
me.

Abe (*fishing in his mail pouch*)

Yes.

Seth

Hello, Mr. Speed.

Josh

How are you, Mr. Gale?

Abe

Here you are, Seth.

(*He hands him a letter.* Seth *takes it to the
right, sits down and starts to read.*)

Josh

I've got to get home to Springfield, Abe, but I'll
be down again in a week or so.

Abe

I'll be here, Josh.

(Josh *goes.* Abe *sits down again at the right, picks up his paper, but doesn't read it.* Ben *stands up and comes down a bit unsteadily.*)

Ben (*angrily*)

Are you going to do it, Abe? Are you goin' to let them make you into a *candidate?*

Abe

I ain't had time to think about it yet.

Ben

Well—I tell you to stop thinkin' before it's too late. Don't let 'em get you. Don't let 'em put you in a store suit that's the uniform of degradation in this miserable country. You're an honest man, Abe Lincoln. You're a good-for-nothin', debt-ridden loafer—but you're an honest man. And you have no place in that den of thieves that's called gov'ment. They'll corrupt you as they've corrupted the whole damn United States. Look at Washington, look at Jefferson, and John Adams—(*He points grandly to the pictures.*)—where are they today? Dead! And everything they stood for and fought for and *won*—that's dead too.

(Ann *comes in to collect the mugs from the table at the left.* Abe *looks at her.*) Why—we'd be better off if we was all black niggers held in the bonds of slavery. *They* get fed—*they* get looked after when they're old and sick. (ANN *goes.*) But *you* don't care—you ain't listenin' to me, neither . . . (*He starts slowly toward the door.*)

ABE

Of course I'm listening, Ben.

BEN

No, you ain't. *I* know. You're goin' to the assembly and join the wolves who're feedin' off the carcass of Liberty. (*He goes out.*)

ABE

You needn't worry. I'm not going.
(ANN *comes in. She crosses to the right to pick up the glasses. She seems extremely subdued.* ABE *looks at her, curiously.*)

ABE

Bowling Green said to tell you he'd be back later, to pay you what he owes.

ANN (*curtly*)

That's all right.
(ANN *puts the glasses and bottle on a tray and picks it up.* ABE *jumps to his feet.*)

ABE

Here, Ann. Let me take that.

ANN (*irritably*)

No—leave it alone! I can carry it! (*She starts across to the left.*)

ABE

Excuse me, Ann. . . .

ANN (*stopping*)

Well?

ABE

Would you come back after you're finished with that? I—I'd like to talk to you.

(SETH *has finished the letter. Its contents seem to have depressed him.*)

ANN

All right. I'll talk to you—if you want.

(*She goes out.* SETH *crosses toward* ABE, *who, during the subsequent dialogue, is continually looking toward the kitchen.*)

SETH

Abe . . . Abe—I got a letter from my folks back in Maryland. It means—I guess I've got to give up the dream we had of moving out into Nebraska territory.

ABE

What's happened, Seth?

SETH (*despondently*)

Well—for one thing, the old man's took sick, and he's pretty feeble.

ABE

I'm sorry to hear that.

SETH

So am I. They've sent for me to come back and work the farm. Measly little thirty-six acres— sandy soil. I tell you, Abe, it's a bitter disappointment to me, when I had my heart all set on going out into the West. And the worst of it is—I'm letting *you* down on it, too.

ABE (*with a glance toward the kitchen*)

Don't think about that, Seth. Maybe I won't be able to move for a while myself. And when your father gets to feeling better, you'll come back . . .

SETH

He won't get to feeling better. Not at his age. I'll be stuck there, just like he was. I'll be pushed in and cramped all the rest of my life, till the malaria gets me, too. . . . Well—there's no use crying about it. If I've got to go back East, I've got to go. (ANN *comes back.*) I'll tell you goodbye, Abe, before I leave.

(*He goes.* ABE *turns and looks at* ANN, *and she at him.*)

ANN

Well—what is it, Abe?

ABE (*rising*)

I just thought—you might like to talk to me.

ANN (*sharply*)

What about?

ABE

That letter you got from New York State.

ANN

What do *you* know about that letter?

ABE

I'm the postmaster. I know more than I ought to about people's private affairs. I couldn't help seeing that that was the handwriting of Mr. Mc-Niel. And I couldn't help seeing, from the look on your face, that the bad news you've been afraid of has come.

(ANN *looks at him with surprise. He is a lot more observant than she had thought.*)

ANN

Whatever the letter said, it's no concern of yours, Abe.

ABE

I know that, Ann. But—it appears to me that you've been crying—and it makes me sad to think that something could have hurt you. The thing is —I think quite a lot of you—always have—ever since I first came here, and met you. I wouldn't mention it, only when you're distressed about something it's a comfort sometimes to find a pair of ears to pour your troubles into—and the Lord knows my ears are big enough to hold a lot.

(*Her attitude of hostility softens and she rewards him with a tender smile.*)

ANN

You're a Christian gentleman, Abe Lincoln. (*She sits down.*)

ABE

No, I ain't. I'm a plain, common sucker with a shirt-tail so short I can't sit on it.

ANN (*laughs*)

Well—sit down, anyway, Abe—here, by me.

ABE

Why—it'd be a pleasure. (*He crosses and sits near her.*)

ANN

You can always say something to make a person laugh, can't you?

ABE

Well—I don't even have to *say* anything. A person just has to *look* at me.

ANN

You're right about that letter, Abe. It's the first I've heard from him in months—and now he says he's delayed by family troubles and doesn't know when he'll be able to get to New Salem again. By which he probably means—never.

ABE

I wouldn't say that, Ann.

ANN

I would. (*She looks at him.*) I reckon you

think I'm a silly fool for ever having promised myself to Mr. McNiel.

ABE

I think no such thing. I liked him myself, and still do, and whatever reasons he had for changing his name I'm sure were honorable. He's a smart man, and a handsome one—and I—I wouldn't blame any girl for—loving him.

ANN (*too emphatically*)

I guess I don't love him, Abe. I guess I couldn't love anybody that was as—as faithless as that.

ABE (*trying to appear unconcerned*)

Well, then. There's nothing to fret about. Now —poor Seth Gale—he got some *really* bad news. His father's sick and he has to give up his dream which was to go and settle out west.

ANN (*looks at him*)

I don't believe you know much about females, Abe.

ABE

Probably I don't—although I certainly spend enough time thinking about 'em.

ANN

You're a big man, and you can lick anybody, and you can't understand the feelings of somebody who is weak. But—I'm a female, and I can't help thinking what they'll be saying about me—all the old gossips, all over town. They'll make it out that he deserted me; I'm a rejected woman. They'll give me their sympathy to my face, but they'll snigger at me behind my back. (*She rises and crosses toward the right.*)

ABE

Yes—that's just about what they would do. But —would you let *them* disturb you?

ANN (*rising*)

I told you—it's just weakness—it's just vanity. It's something you couldn't understand, Abe.

(*She has crossed to the window and is staring out.* ABE *twists in his chair to look at her.*)

ABE

Maybe I can understand it, Ann. I've got a kind of vanity myself. Josh Speed said so, and he's right. . . . It's—it's nothing but vanity that's kept me from declaring my inclinations toward you.

(*She turns, amazed, and looks at him.*)
You see, I don't like to be sniggered at, either. I know what I am—and I know what I look like—and I know that I've got nothing to offer any girl that I'd be in love with.

ANN

Are you saying that you'rs in love with me, Abe?

ABE (*with deep earnestness*)

Yes—I am saying that.

(*He stands up, facing her. She looks intently into his eyes.*)

I've been loving you—a long time—with all my heart. You see, Ann—you're a particularly fine girl. You've got sense, and you've got bravery— those are two things that I admire particularly. And you're powerful good to look at, too. So—it's only natural I should have a great regard for you. But—I don't mean to worry you about it, Ann. I only mentioned it because—if you would do me the honor of keeping company with me for a while, it might shut the old gossips' mouths. They'd figure you'd chucked McNiel for—for some one else. Even me.

ANN (*going to him*)

I thought I knew you pretty well, Abe. But I didn't.

ABE (*worried*)

Why do you say that? Do you consider I was too forward, in speaking out as I did?

ANN (*gravely*)

No, Abe. . . . I've always thought a lot of you —the way I thought you were. But—the idea of love between you and me—I can't say how I feel about that, because now you're like some other person, that I'm meeting for the first time.

ABE (*quietly*)

I'm not expecting you to feel anything for me. I'd never dream of expecting such a thing.

Ann

I know that, Abe. You'd be willing to give everything you have and never expect anything in return. Maybe you're different in that way from any man I've ever heard of. And I can tell you this much—now, and truthfully—if I ever do love you, I'll be happy about it—and lucky, to be loving a good, decent man. . . . If you just give me time—to think about it. . . .

Abe (*unable to believe his eyes and ears*)

You mean—if you took time—you might get in your heart something like the feeling I have for you?

Ann (*with great tenderness*)

I don't know, Abe. (*She clutches his lapel.*) But I do know that you're a man who could fill any one's heart—yes, fill it and warm it and make it glad to be living.

(Abe *covers her hand with his.*)

Abe

Ann—I've always tried hard to believe what the orators tell us—that this is a land of equal opportunity for all. But I've never been able to credit it, any more than I could agree that God made all men in his own image. But—if I could win you, Ann—I'd be willing to disbelieve everything I've ever seen with my own eyes, and have faith in everything wonderful that I've ever read in poetry books.

(*Both are silent for a moment. Then* ANN *turns away.*)

But—I'm not asking you to say anything now. And I won't ask you until the day comes when I know I've got a right to. (*He turns and walks quickly toward the door, picking up his mail pouch.*)

ANN

Abe! Where are you going?

ABE

I'm going to find Bowling Green and tell him a good joke. (*He grins. He is standing in the door-way.*)

ANN

A *joke?* What about?

ABE

I'm going to tell him that I'm a candidate for the assembly of the State of Illinois. (*He goes.*)

(*The light fades.*)

END OF SCENE II

SCENE III

Bowling Green's house near New Salem.

It is a small room, but the walls are lined with books and family pictures. In the center is a table with a lamp on it. Another light—a candle in a glass globe—is on a bureau at the right. There are comfortable chairs on either side of the table, and a sofa at the left.

At the back, toward the left, is the front door. A rifle is leaning against the wall by the door. There is another door in the right wall. Toward the right, at the back, is a ladder fixed against the wall leading up through an opening to the attic.

It is late in the evening, a year or so after Scene II. A storm is raging outside.

BOWLING *is reading aloud from a sort of pamphlet. His comfortable wife,* NANCY, *is listening and sewing.*

BOWLING

"And how much more interesting did the spectacle become when, starting into full life and animation, as a simultaneous call for 'Pickwick' burst from his followers, that illustrious man slowly mounted into the Windsor chair, on which he had been previously seated, and addressed the club himself had founded."

(BOWLING *chuckles.* NANCY *laughs.*)

NANCY

He sounds precisely like *you*, Bowling.
(*There is a knock at the door.*)

NANCY (*nervous*)

That's not Abe's knock. Who can it be?

BOWLING (*rising*)

We don't know yet, my dear.

NANCY

It's a strange hour for any one to be calling.
You'd better have that gun ready.
(BOWLING *unbolts and opens the door. It is*
JOSH SPEED.)

BOWLING

Why—Josh Speed!

JOSH

Good evening, Bowling.

BOWLING

We haven't seen you in a coon's age.

NANCY

Good evening, Mr. Speed.

JOSH

Good evening, Mrs. Green. And I beg you to forgive me for this untimely intrusion.

NANCY

We're delighted to see you. Take your wrap off.

Josh

Thank you. I've just come down from Springfield. I heard Abe Lincoln was in town and I was told I might find him here.

Bowling

He's been sleeping here, up in the attic.

Nancy

But he's out now at the Rutledge Farm, tending poor little Ann.

Josh

Miss Rutledge? What's the matter with her?

Nancy

She's been taken with the brain sickness. It's the most shocking thing. People have been dying from it right and left.

Bowling

But Ann's young. She'll pull through, all right. Sit down, Josh.

Josh

Thank you.

(*He sits.* **Bowling** *places the pamphlet on the top of the bookcase and stands there, filling his pipe.*)

Nancy

I suppose you know that Abe came rushing down from Vandalia the moment he heard she was taken. He's deeply in love with her.

BOWLING

Now, Nancy—don't exaggerate.
(JOSH *is listening to all this, intently.*)

JOSH

So Abe is in love. I wondered what has been the
matter with him lately.

NANCY

Why, it's written all over his poor, homely face.

JOSH

The last time I saw him, he seemed pretty
moody. But when I asked him what was wrong, he
said it was his liver.

BOWLING (*laughing*)

That sounds more likely. Has he been getting
on well in the Assembly?

JOSH

No. He has just been sitting there—drawing his
three dollars a day—and taking no apparent interest in the proceedings. Do you fancy that Miss
Rutledge cares anything for him?

NANCY

Indeed she does! She broke her promise to that
Mr. McNiel because of her feelings for Abe!

JOSH

Has he any notion of marrying her?

NANCY

It's the only notion of his life right now. And the sooner they are married, the better for both of them.

BOWLING (*seating himself*)

Better for her, perhaps—but the worse for him.

NANCY (*finishing her sewing*)

And why? The Rutledges are fine people, superior in every way to those riff-raff Hankses and Lincolns that are Abe's family!

BOWLING

I think you feel as I do, Josh. Abe has his own way to go and—sweet and pretty as Ann undoubtedly is—she'd only be a hindrance to him.

JOSH

I guess it wouldn't matter much if she could give him a little of the happiness he's never had.

NANCY (*rising*)

That's just it! I think as much of Abe as you do, Bowling. But we can't deny that he's a poor man, and he's failed in trade, and he's been in the legislature for a year without accomplishing a blessed thing . . . (*She goes to the bookcase to put her sewing-basket away.*)

BOWLING

He could go to Springfield and set up a law practice and make a good thing of it. Ninian Ed-

wards would help him to get started. And he'd soon
forget little Ann. He has just happened to fasten
on her his own romantic ideal of what's beautiful
and unattainable. Let him ever attain her, and
she'd break his heart.

NANCY (*seating herself*)

Do you agree with Bowling on that, Mr. Speed?

JOSH (*sadly*)

I can't say, Mrs. Green. I've abandoned the
attempt to predict anything about Abe Lincoln.
The first time I ever saw him was when he was
piloting that steamboat, the *Talisman*. You remember how she ran into trouble at the dam. I had
a valuable load of goods aboard for my father's
store, and I was sure that steamboat, goods and
all were a total loss. But Abe got her through. It
was a great piece of work. I thought, "Here is a
reliable man." So I cultivated his acquaintance,
believing, in my conceit, that I could help him to
fame and fortune. I soon learned differently. I
found out that he has plenty of strength and courage in his body—but in his mind he's a hopeless
hypochondriac. He can split rails, push a plough,
crack jokes, all day—and then sit up all night reading "Hamlet" and brooding over his own fancied
resemblance to that melancholy prince. Maybe he's
a great philosopher—maybe he's a great fool. I
don't know what he is.

BOWLING (*laughs*)

Well—if only Ann had sense enough to see all the things *you* saw, Josh, she'd be so terrified of him she'd run all the way back to York State and find McNiel. At least, *he's* not complicated.

NANCY (*with deeper emotion*)

You're talking about Abe Lincoln as if he were some problem that you found in a book, and it's interesting to try to figure it out. Well—maybe he is a problem—but he's also a man, and a miserable one. And what do you do for his misery? You laugh at his comical jokes and you vote for him on election day and give him board and lodging when he needs it. But all that doesn't give a scrap of satisfaction to Abe's soul—and never will. Because the one thing he needs is a woman with the will to face life for him.

BOWLING

You think he's afraid to face it himself?

NANCY

He is! He listens too much to the whispers, that he heard in the forest where he grew up, and where he always goes now when he wants to be alone. They're the whispers of the women behind him— his dead mother—and *her* mother, who was no better than she should be. He's got that awful fear on him, of not knowing what the whispers mean, or where they're directing him. And none of your back-slapping will knock that fear out of him. Only a woman can free him—a woman who loves him truly, and believes in him. . . .

(*There is a knock on the door.*)

BOWLING

That's Abe now. (*He gets up and opens it.*)

(ABE *is there, bareheaded, wet by the storm. He now wears a fairly respectable dark suit of clothes. He looks older and grimmer.*)

BOWLING

Why, hello, Abe! We've been sitting up waiting for you. Come on in out of the wet!

(ABE *comes in.* BOWLING *shuts the door behind him.*)

NANCY

We were reading The Posthumous Papers of the Pickwick Club when Mr. Speed came in.

ABE

Hello, Josh. Glad to see you.

JOSH

Hello, Abe.

(ABE *turns to* NANCY.)

ABE

Nancy . . .

NANCY

Yes, Abe?

ABE

She's dead.

BOWLING

Ann? She's dead?

ABE

Yes. Tonight, the fever suddenly got worse.
They couldn't seem to do anything for it.

(NANCY *gives* BOWLING *a swift look, then goes
quickly to* ABE *and takes his hand.*)

NANCY

Oh, Abe—I'm so sorry. She was such a dear little
girl. Every one who knew her will join in mourn-
ing for her.

ABE

I know they will. But it won't do any good. She's
dead.

BOWLING

Sit down, Abe, and rest yourself.

ABE

No—I'm not fit company for anybody. I'd better be going. (*He turns toward the door.*)

JOSH (*stopping him*)

No, you don't, Abe. You'll stay right here.

BOWLING

You better do what Josh tells you.

NANCY

Come here, Abe. Please sit down.

(ABE *looks from one to the other, then obedi-
ently goes to a chair and sits.*)

Your bed is ready for you upstairs when you
want it.

ABE (*dully*)

You're the best friends I've got in the world,
and it seems a pretty poor way to reward you for
all that you've given me, to come here now, and in-
flict you with a corpse.

BOWLING

This is your home, Abe. This is where you're
loved.

ABE

Yes, that's right. And I love you, Bowling and
Nancy. But I loved her more than everything else
that I've ever known.

NANCY

I know you did, Abe. I know it.

ABE

I used to think it was better to be alone. I was
always most contented when I was alone. I had
queer notions that if you got too close to people,
you could see the truth about them, that behind
the surface, they're all insane, and they could see
the same in you. And then—when I saw her, I knew
there could be beauty and purity in people—like
the purity you sometimes see in the sky at night.
When I took hold of her hand, and held it, all fear,
all doubt, went out of me. I believed in God. I'd
have been glad to work for her until I die, to get

for her everything out of life that she wanted. If
she thought I could do it, then I could. That was
my belief. . . . And then I had to stand there, as
helpless as a twig in a whirlpool; I had to stand
there and watch her die. And her father and mother
were there, too, praying to God for her soul. The
Lord giveth, and the Lord taketh away, blessed be
the name of the Lord! That's what they kept on
saying. But I couldn't pray with them. I couldn't
give any devotion to one who has the power of
death, and uses it. (*He has stood up, and is speaking with more passion.*) I'm making a poor exhibition of myself—and I'm sorry—but—I can't
stand it. I can't live with myself any longer. I've
got to die and be with her again, or I'll go crazy!
(*He goes to the door and opens it. The storm con-
tinues.*) I can't bear to think of her out there
alone!

(NANCY *looks at* BOWLING *with frantic appeal.
He goes to* ABE, *who is standing in the doorway,
looking out.*)

BOWLING (*with great tenderness*)

Abe . . . I want you to go upstairs and see if you
can't get some sleep. . . . Please, Abe—as a special
favor to Nancy and me.

ABE (*after a moment*)

All right, Bowling. (*He turns and goes to the
ladder.*)

NANCY

Here's a light for you, dear Abe. (*She hands him the candle.*)

ABE

Thank you, Nancy. . . . Good night. (*He goes up the ladder into the attic.*)

(*They all look up after him.*)

NANCY (*tearful*)

Poor, lonely soul.

(BOWLING *cautions her to be quiet.*)

JOSH

Keep him here with you, Mrs. Green. Don't let him out of your sight.

BOWLING

We won't, Josh.

JOSH

Good night. (*He picks up his hat and cloak and goes.*)

BOWLING

Good night, Josh. (*He closes and bolts the door, then comes down to the table and picks up the lamp.*)

(NANCY *looks up once more, then goes out at the right.* BOWLING *follows her out, carrying the lamp with him. He closes the door behind him, so that the only light on the stage is the beam from the attic.*)

CURTAIN

END OF ACT ONE

ACT II

ACT II

SCENE IV

Law office of Stuart and Lincoln on the second floor of the Court House in Springfield, Ill. A sunny summer's afternoon, some five years after the preceding scene.

The room is small, with two windows and one door, upstage, which leads to the hall and staircase.

At the right is a table and chair, at the left an old desk, littered with papers. At the back is a ramshackle bed, with a buffalo robe thrown over it. Below the windows are some rough shelves, sagging with law books. There is an old wood stove.

On the wall above the desk is hung an American flag, with 26 stars. Between the windows is an election poster, for Harrison and Tyler, with a list of Electors, the last of whom is Ab'm Lincoln, of Sangamon.

Billy Herndon is working at the table. He is young, slight, serious-minded, smouldering. He looks up as Abe comes in. Abe wears a battered plug hat, a light alpaca coat, and carries an ancient, threadbare carpet-bag. He is evidently not in a talkative mood. His boots are caked in mud.

65

He is only thirty-one years old, but his youth was buried with Ann Rutledge.

He leaves the office door open, and lettered on it we see the number, 4, and the firm's name—Stuart & Lincoln, Attorneys & Counsellors at Law.

BILLY

How de do, Mr. Lincoln. Glad to see you back.

ABE

Good day, Billy. (*He sets down the carpet-bag, takes off his hat and puts it on his desk.*)

BILLY

How was it on the circuit, Mr. Lincoln?

ABE

About as usual.

BILLY

Have you been keeping in good health?

ABE

Not particularly. But Doc Henry dosed me enough to keep me going. (*He sits down at the desk and starts looking at letters and papers that have accumulated during his absence. He takes little interest in them, pigeonholing some letters unopened.*)

BILLY

Did you have occasion to make any political speeches?

ABE

Oh—they got me up on the stump a couple of times. Ran into Stephen Douglas—he was out campaigning, of course—and we had some argument in public.

BILLY (*greatly interested*)

That's good! What issues did you and Mr. Douglas discuss?

ABE

Now—don't get excited, Billy. We weren't taking it serious. There was no blood shed. . . . What's the news here?

BILLY

Judge Stuart wrote that he arrived safely in Washington and the campaign there is getting almost as hot as the weather. Mrs. Fraim stopped in to say she couldn't possibly pay your fee for a while.

ABE

I should hope not. I ought to be paying her, seeing as I defended her poor husband and he hanged.

(BILLY *hands him a letter and watches him intently, while he reads it.*)

BILLY

That was left here by hand, and I promised to call it especially to your attention. It's from the Elijah P. Lovejoy League of Freemen. They want you to speak at an Abolitionist rally next Thursday evening. It'll be a very important affair.

ABE (*reflectively*)

It's funny, Billy—I was thinking about Lovejoy the other day—trying to figure what it is in a man that makes him glad to be a martyr. I was on the boat coming from Quincy to Alton, and there was a gentleman on board with twelve Negroes. He was shipping them down to Vicksburg for sale— had 'em chained six and six together. Each of them had a small iron clevis around his wrist, and this was chained to the main chain, so that those Negroes were strung together precisely like fish on a trot line. I gathered they were being separated forever from their homes—mothers, fathers, wives, children—whatever families the poor creatures had got—going to be whipped into perpetual slavery, and no questions asked. It was quite a shocking sight.

BILLY (*excited*)

Then you will give a speech at the Lovejoy rally?

ABE (*wearily*)

I doubt it. That Freemen's League is a pack of hell-roaring fanatics. Talk reason to them and they scorn you for being a mealy-mouth. Let 'em make their own noise. (ABE *has opened a letter. He starts to read it.*)

(BILLY *looks at him with resentful disappointment, but he knows too well that any argument would be futile. He resumes his work. After a moment,* BOWLING GREEN *comes in, followed by* JOSH SPEED.)

BOWLING

Are we interrupting the majesty of the Law?

ABE (*heartily*)

Bowling! (*He jumps up and grasps* BOWLING'S *hand.*) How are you, Bowling?

BOWLING

Tolerably well, Abe—and glad to see you.

ABE

This is Billy Herndon—Squire Green, of New Salem. Hello, Josh.

JOSH

Hello, Abe.

BILLY (*shaking hands with* BOWLING)

I'm proud to know you, sir. Mr. Lincoln speaks of you constantly.

BOWLING

Thank you, Mr. Herndon. Are you a lawyer, too?

BILLY (*seriously*)

I hope to be, sir. I'm serving here as a clerk in Judge Stuart's absence.

BOWLING

So now you're teaching others, Abe?

ABE

Just providing a bad example.

BOWLING

I can believe it. Look at the mess on that desk.
Shameful!

ABE

Give me another year of law practise and I'll
need a warehouse for the overflow. . . . But—sit
yourself down, Bowling, and tell me what brings
you to Springfield.

(BOWLING *sits.* JOSH *has sat on the couch,
smoking his pipe.* BILLY *is again at the table.*)

BOWLING

I've been up to Lake Michigan—fishing—came in
today on the steam-cars—scared me out of a year's
growth. But how are you doing, Abe? Josh says
you're still broke, but you're a great social success.

ABE

True—on both counts. I'm greatly in demand
at all the more elegant functions. You remember
Ninian Edwards?

BOWLING

Of course.

ABE

Well, sir—I'm a guest at his mansion regularly.
He's got a house so big you could race horses in
the parlor. And his wife is one of the Todd family
from Kentucky. Very high-grade people. They
spell their name with two D's—which is pretty impressive when you consider that one was enough
for God.

JOSH

Tell Bowling whom you met over in Rochester.

ABE

The President of the United States!

BOWLING

You don't tell me so!

ABE

Do you see that hand? (*He holds out his right hand, palm upward.*)

BOWLING

Yes—I see it.

ABE

It has shaken the hand of Martin Van Buren!

BOWLING (*laughing*)

Was the President properly respectful to you, Abe?

ABE

Indeed he was! He said to me, "We've been hearing great things of you in Washington." I found out later he'd said the same thing to every other cross-roads politician he'd met. (*He laughs.*) But Billy Herndon there is pretty disgusted with me for associating with the wrong kind of people. Billy's a firebrand—a real, radical abolitionist—and he can't stand anybody who keeps his mouth shut and abides by the Constitution. If he had his way, the whole Union would be set on fire and we'd all be burned to a crisp. Eh, Billy?

BILLY (*grimly*)

Yes, Mr. Lincoln. And if you'll permit me to say so, I think you'd be of more use to your fellow-men if you allowed some of the same incendiary impulses to come out in you.

ABE

You see, Bowling? He wants me to get down into the blood-soaked arena and grapple with all the lions of injustice and oppression.

BOWLING

Mr. Herndon—my profound compliments.

BILLY (*rising and taking his hat*)

Thank you, sir. (*He shakes hands with* BOWLING, *then turns to* ABE:) I have the writ prepared in the Willcox case. I'll take it down to the Clerk of Court to be attested.

ABE

All right, Billy.

BILLY (*to* BOWLING)

Squire Green—Mr. Lincoln regards you and Mr. Speed as the best friends he has on earth, and I should like to beg you, in his presence, for God's sake drag him out of this stagnant pool in which he's rapidly drowning himself. Good day, sir—good day, Mr. Speed.

Josh

Good day, Billy.
(Billy *has gone*.)

Bowling

That's a bright young man, Abe. Seems to have a good grasp of things.

Abe (*looking after* Billy)

He's going downstairs to the Clerk's office, but he took his hat. Which means that before he comes back to work, he'll have paid a little visit to the Chenery House saloon.

Bowling

Does the boy drink?

Abe

Yes. He's got great fires in him, but he's putting 'em out fast. . . . Now—tell me about New Salem. (*He leans against the wall near the window.*)

Bowling

Practically nothing of it left.

Abe

How's that blessed wife of yours?

Bowling

Nancy's busier than ever, and more than ever concerned about your innermost thoughts and yearnings. In fact, she instructed me expressly to ask what on earth is the matter with you?

ABE (*laughs*)

You can tell her there's nothing the matter. I've been able to pay off my debts to the extent of some seven cents on the dollar, and I'm sound of skin and skeleton.

BOWLING

But why don't we hear more from you and of you?

ABE

Josh can tell you. I've been busy.

BOWLING

What at?

ABE

I'm a candidate.

JOSH (*pointing to the poster*)

Haven't you noticed his name? It's here—at the bottom of the list of Electors on the Whig ticket.

ABE

Yes, sir—if old Tippecanoe wins next fall, I'll be a member of the Electoral College.

BOWLING

The Electoral College! And is that the best you can do?

ABE

Yes—in the limited time at my disposal. I had a letter from Seth Gale—remember—he used to live in New Salem and was always aiming to move West. He's settled down in Maryland now and has a wife

and a son. He says that back East they're powerful worried about the annexation of Texas.

BOWLING

They have reason to be. It would probably mean
extending slavery through all the territories, from
Kansas and Nebraska right out to Oregon and
California. That would give the South absolute
rule of the country—and God help the rest of us in
the free states.

JOSH

It's an ugly situation, all right. It's got the
seeds in it of nothing more nor less than civil war.

ABE

Well, if so, it'll be the abolitionists' own fault.
They know where this trouble might lead, and yet
they go right on agitating. They ought to be
locked up for disturbing the peace, all of them.

BOWLING

I thought you were opposed to slavery, Abe.
Have you changed your mind about it?

ABE (*ambles over to the couch and sprawls on it*)

No. I am opposed to slavery. But I'm even more
opposed to going to war. And, on top of that, I
know what you're getting at, both of you. (*He
speaks to them with the utmost good nature.*)
You're following Billy Herndon's lead—troubling

your kind hearts with concerns about me and when am I going to amount to something. Is that it?

BOWLING

Oh, no, Abe. Far be it from me to interfere in your life.

JOSH

Or me, either. If we happen to feel that, so far, you've been a big disappointment to us, we'll surely keep it to ourselves.

ABE (*laughs*)

I'm afraid you'll have to do what I've had to do —which is, learn to accept me for what I am. I'm no fighting man. I found that out when I went through the Black Hawk War, and was terrified that I might have to fire a shot at an Indian. Fortunately, the Indians felt the same way, so I never saw one of them. Now, I know plenty of men who like to fight; they're willing to kill, and not scared of being killed. All right. Let them attend to the battles that have to be fought.

BOWLING

Peaceable men have sometimes been of service to their country.

ABE

They may have been peaceable when they started, but they didn't remain so long after they'd become mixed in the great brawl of politics. (*He sits up.*) Suppose I ran for Congress, and got elected.

I'd be right in the thick of that ugly situation you were speaking of. One day I might have to cast my vote on the terrible issue of war or peace. It might be war with Mexico over Texas; or war with England over Oregon; or even war with our own people across the Ohio River. What attitude would I take in deciding which way to vote? "The Liberal attitude," of course. And what is the Liberal attitude? To go to war, for a tract of land, or a moral principle? Or to avoid war at all costs? No, sir. The place for me is in the Electoral College, where all I have to do is vote for the President whom everybody else elected four months previous.

BOWLING

Well, Abe—you were always an artful dodger— and maybe you'll be able to go on to the end of your days avoiding the clutch of your own conscience.

(NINIAN EDWARDS *comes in. He is a little stouter and more prosperous.*)

ABE—JOSH

Hello, Ninian.

NINIAN

Hello. I saw Billy Herndon at the Chenery House and he said you were back from the circuit. (*He sees* BOWLING.) Why—it's my good friend Squire Green. How de do, and welcome to Springfield. (*He shakes hands with* BOWLING.)

BOWLING

Thank you, Mr. Edwards.

NINIAN

I just called in, Abe, to tell you you must dine with us. And, Squire, Mrs. Edwards would be honored to receive you, if your engagements will permit—and you, too, Josh.

JOSH

Delighted!

NINIAN

We're proudly exhibiting my sister-in-law, Miss Mary Todd, who has just come from Kentucky to grace our home. She's a very gay young lady—speaks French like a native, recites poetry at the drop of a hat, and knows the names and habits of all the flowers. I've asked Steve Douglas and some of the other eligibles to meet her, so you boys had better get in early.

BOWLING

My compliments to Mrs. Edwards, but my own poor wife awaits me impatiently, I hope.

NINIAN

I appreciate your motives, Squire, and applaud them. You'll be along presently, Abe?

ABE

I wouldn't be surprised.

NINIAN

Good. You'll meet a delightful young lady. And

I'd better warn you she's going to survey the whole
field of matrimonial prospects and select the one
who promises the most. So you'd better be on your
guard, Abe, unless you're prepared to lose your
standing as a free man.

ABE

I thank you for the warning, Ninian.

NINIAN

Good day to you, Squire. See you later, Josh.
(*He goes out.*)

ABE

There, Bowling—you see how things are with me.
Hardly a day goes by but what I'm invited to meet
some eager young female who has all the graces, including an ability to speak the language of diplo-
macy.

BOWLING

I'm sorry, Abe, that I shan't be able to hear
you carrying on a flirtation in French.

(ABE *looks at him, curiously.*)

ABE

I'm not pretending with you, Bowling—or you,
Josh. I couldn't fool you any better than I can
fool myself. I know what you're thinking about
me, and I think so, too. Only I'm not so merci-
ful in considering my own shortcomings, or so
ready to forgive them, as you are. But—you talk
about civil war—there seems to be one going on

inside me all the time. Both sides are right and both are wrong and equal in strength. I'd like to be able to rise superior to the struggle—but—it says in the Bible that a house divided against itself cannot stand, so I reckon there's not much hope. One of these days, I'll just split asunder, and part company with myself—and it'll be a good riddance from both points of view. However—come on. (*He takes his hat.*) You've got to get back to Nancy, and Josh and I have got to make a good impression upon Miss Mary Todd, of Kentucky. (*He waves them to the door. As they go out, the light fades.*)

END OF SCENE IV

SCENE V

Parlor of the Edwards house in Springfield. An evening in November, some six months after the preceding scene.

There is a fireplace at the right, a heavily curtained bay window at the left, a door at the back leading into the front hall.

At the right, by the fireplace, are a small couch and an easy chair. There is another couch at the left, and a table and chairs at the back. There are family portraits on the walls. It is all moderately elegant.

NINIAN is standing before the fire, in conversation with ELIZABETH, his wife. She is high-bred, ladylike—excessively so. She is, at the moment, in a state of some agitation.

ELIZABETH

I cannot believe it! It is an outrageous reflection on my sister's good sense.

NINIAN

I'm not so sure of that. Mary has known Abe for several months, and she has had plenty of chance to observe him closely.

ELIZABETH

She has been entertained by him, as we all have.

But she has been far more attentive to Edwin Webb and Stephen Douglas and many others who are distinctly eligible.

NINIAN

Isn't it remotely possible that she sees more in Abe than you do?

ELIZABETH

Nonsense! Mr. Lincoln's chief virtue is that he hides no part of his simple soul from any one. He's a most amiable creature, to be sure; but as the husband of a high-bred, high-spirited young lady . . .

NINIAN

Quite so, Elizabeth. Mary *is* high-spirited! That is just why she set her cap for him.

(ELIZABETH *looks at him sharply, then laughs.*)

ELIZABETH

You're making fun of me, Ninian. You're deliberately provoking me into becoming excited about nothing.

NINIAN

No, Elizabeth—I am merely trying to prepare you for a rude shock. You think Abe Lincoln would be overjoyed to capture an elegant, cultivated girl, daughter of the President of the Bank of Kentucky, descendant of a long line of English gentlemen. Well, you are mistaken . . .

(MARY TODD *comes in. She is twenty-two—short, pretty, remarkably sharp. She stops short in the*

doorway, and her suspecting eyes dart from ELIZA-
BETH *to* NINIAN.)

MARY

What were you two talking about?

NINIAN

I was telling your sister about the new song the
boys are singing:
"What is the great commotion, motion,
  Our country through?
  It is the ball a-rolling on
  For Tippecanoe and Tyler, too—for Tippe-
    canoe . . ."

MARY (*with a rather grim smile*)

I compliment you for thinking quickly, Ninian.
But you were talking about *me!* (*She looks at*
ELIZABETH, *who quails a little before her sister's
determination.*) Weren't you?

ELIZABETH

Yes, Mary, we were.

MARY

And quite seriously, I gather.

NINIAN

I'm afraid that our dear Elizabeth has become
unduly alarmed . . .

ELIZABETH (*snapping at him*)

Let me say what I have to say! (*She turns to*
MARY.) Mary—you must tell me the truth. Are

you—have you ever given one moment's serious thought to the possibility of marriage with Abraham Lincoln?

(MARY *looks at each of them, her eyes flashing.*) I promise you, Mary, that to me such a notion is too far beyond the bounds of credibility to be . . .

MARY

But Ninian has raised the horrid subject, hasn't he? He has brought the evil scandal out into the open, and we must face it, fearlessly. Let us do so at once, by all means. I shall answer you, Elizabeth: I have given more than one moment's thought to the possibility you mentioned—and I have decided that I shall be Mrs. Lincoln. (*She seats herself on the couch.*)

(NINIAN *is about to say, "I told you so," but thinks better of it.* ELIZABETH *can only gasp and gape.*)

I have examined, carefully, the qualifications of all the young gentlemen, and some of the old ones, in this neighborhood. Those of Mr. Lincoln seem to me superior to all others, and he is my choice.

ELIZABETH

Do you expect me to congratulate you upon this amazing selection?

MARY

No! I ask for no congratulations, nor condolences, either.

ELIZABETH (*turning away*)

Then I shall offer none.

NINIAN

Forgive me for prying, Mary—but have you as yet communicated your decision to the gentleman himself?

MARY (*with a slight smile at* NINIAN)

Not yet. But he is coming to call this evening, and he will ask humbly for my hand in marriage; and, after I have displayed the proper amount of surprise and confusion, I shall murmur, timidly, "Yes!"

ELIZABETH (*pitiful*)

You make a brave jest of it, Mary. But as for me, I am deeply and painfully shocked. I don't know what to say to you. But I urge you, I beg you, as your elder sister, responsible to our father and our dead mother for your welfare . . .

MARY (*with a certain tenderness*)

I can assure you, Elizabeth—it is useless to beg or command. I have made up my mind.

NINIAN

I admire your courage, Mary, but I should like . . .

ELIZABETH

I think, Ninian, that this is a matter for discussion solely between my sister and myself!

MARY

No! I want to hear what Ninian has to say. (*To* NINIAN.) What is it?

NINIAN

I only wondered if I might ask you another question.   MARY (*calmly*)

You may.   NINIAN

Understand, my dear—I'm not quarreling with you. My affection for Abe is eternal—but—I'm curious to know—what is it about him that makes you choose him for a husband?

MARY (*betraying her first sign of uncertainty*)

I should like to give you a plain, simple answer, Ninian. But I cannot.

ELIZABETH (*jumping at this*)

Of course you cannot! You're rushing blindly into this. You have no conception of what it will mean to your future.

MARY

You're wrong about that, Elizabeth. This is not the result of wild, tempestuous infatuation. I have not been swept off my feet. Mr. Lincoln is a Westerner, but that is his only point of resemblance to Young Lochinvar. I simply feel that of all the men I've ever known, he is the one whose life and destiny I want most to share.

ELIZABETH

Haven't you sense enough to know you could never be happy with him? His breeding—his background—his manner—his whole point of view . . . ?

MARY (*gravely*)

I could not be content with a "happy" marriage in the accepted sense of the word. I have no craving for comfort and security.

ELIZABETH

And have you a craving for the kind of life you would lead? A miserable cabin, without a servant, without a stitch of clothing that is fit for exhibition in decent society?

MARY (*raising her voice*)

I have not yet tried poverty, so I cannot say how I should take to it. But I might well prefer it to anything I have previously known—so long as there is forever before me the chance for high adventure—so long as I can know that I am always going forward, with my husband, along a road that leads across the horizon. (*This last is said with a sort of mad intensity.*)

ELIZABETH

And how far do you think you will go with any one like Abe Lincoln, who is lazy and shiftless and prefers to stop constantly along the way to tell jokes?

Mary (*rising; furious*)

He will *not* stop, if I am strong enough to make him go on! And I am strong! I know what *you* expect of me. You want me to do precisely as you have done—and marry a man like Ninian—and I know many, that are *just* like him! But with all due respect to my dear brother-in-law—I don't want that—and I won't have it! Never! You live in a house with a fence around it—presumably to prevent the common herd from gaining access to your sacred precincts—but really to prevent you, yourselves, from escaping from your own narrow lives. In Abraham Lincoln I see a man who has split rails for other men's fences, but who will never build one around himself!

Elizabeth

What are you *saying*, Mary? You are talking with a degree of irresponsibility that is not far from sheer madness . . .

Mary (*scornfully*)

I imagine it does seem like insanity to you! You married a man who was settled and established in the world, with a comfortable inheritance, and no problems to face. And you've never made a move to change your condition, or improve it. You consider it couldn't be improved. To you, all this represents perfection. But it doesn't to me! I want the chance to *shape* a new life, for myself, and for my husband. Is that irresponsibility?

(*A* Maid *appears.*)

MAID

Mr. Lincoln, ma'am.

ELIZABETH

He's here.

MARY (*firmly*)

I shall see him!

MAID

Will you step in, Mr. Lincoln?

(Abe *comes in, wearing a new suit, his hair nearly neat.*)

ABE

Good evening, Mrs. Edwards. Good evening, Miss Todd. Ninian, good evening.

ELIZABETH

Good evening.

MARY

Good evening, Mr. Lincoln.

(*She sits on the couch at the left.*)

NINIAN

Glad to see you, Abe.

(Abe *sees that there is electricity in the atmosphere of this parlor. He tries hard to be affably casual.*)

ABE

I'm afraid I'm a little late in arriving, but I ran

into an old friend of mine, wife of Jack Armstrong, the champion rowdy of New Salem. I believe you have some recollection of him, Ninian.

NINIAN (*smiling*)

I most certainly have. What's he been up to now?

ABE (*stands in front of the fireplace*)

Oh, he's all right, but Hannah, his wife, is in fearful trouble because her son Duff is up for murder and she wants me to defend him. I went over to the jail to interview the boy and he looks pretty tolerably guilty to me. But I used to give him lessons in the game of marbles while his mother foxed my pants for me. (*He turns to* ELIZABETH.) That means, she sewed buckskin around the legs of my pants so I wouldn't tear 'em to shreds going through underbrush when I was surveying. Well—in view of old times, I felt I had to take the case and do what I can to obstruct the orderly processes of justice.

NINIAN (*laughs, with some relief*)

And the boy will be acquitted. I tell you, Abe—this country would be law-abiding and peaceful if it weren't for you lawyers. But—if you will excuse Elizabeth and me, we must hear the children's prayers and see them safely abed.

ABE

Why—I'd be glad to hear their prayers, too.

NINIAN

Oh, no! You'd only keep them up till all hours with your stories. Come along, Elizabeth.

(ELIZABETH *doesn't want to go, but doesn't know what to do to prevent it.*)

ABE (*to* ELIZABETH)

Kiss them good night, for me.

NINIAN

We'd better not tell them you're in the house, or they'll be furious.

ELIZABETH (*making one last attempt*)

Mary! Won't you come with us and say good night to the children?

NINIAN

No, my dear. Leave Mary here—to keep Abe entertained. (*He guides* ELIZABETH *out, following her.*)

MARY (*with a little laugh*)

I don't blame Ninian for keeping you away from those children. They all adore you.

ABE

Well—I always seemed to get along well with children. Probably it's because they never want to take me seriously.

MARY

You understand them—that's the important

thing . . . But—do sit down, Mr. Lincoln. (*She indicates that he is to sit next to her.*)

ABE

Thank you—I will. (*He starts to cross to the couch to sit beside* MARY. *She looks at him with melting eyes. The lights fade.*)

END OF SCENE V

SCENE VI

Again the Law Office. It is afternoon of New Year's Day, a few weeks after the preceding scene.

ABE is sitting, slumped in his chair, staring at his desk. He has his hat and overcoat on. A muffler is hanging about his neck, untied.

JOSH SPEED is half-sitting on the table at the right. He is reading a long letter, with most serious attention. At length he finishes it, refolds it very carefully, stares at the floor.

ABE

Have you finished it, Josh?

JOSH

Yes.

ABE

Well—do you think it's all right?

JOSH

No, Abe—I don't.
(ABE *turns slowly and looks at him.*)
I think the sending of this letter would be a most grave mistake—and that is putting it mildly and charitably.

ABE

Have I stated the case too crudely? (ABE *is evidently in a serious state of distress, although*

93

he is making a tremendous effort to disguise it by speaking in what he intends to be a coldly impersonal tone. He is struggling mightily to hold himself back from the brink of nervous collapse.)

JOSH

No—I have no quarrel with your choice of words. None whatever. If anything, the phraseology is too correct. But your method of doing it, Abe! It's brutal, it's heartless, it's so unworthy of you that I—I'm at a loss to understand how you ever thought you could do it this way.

ABE

I've done the same thing before with a woman to whom I seemed to have become attached. She approved of my action.

JOSH

This is a different woman. (*He walks over to the window, then turns again toward* ABE.) You cannot seem to accept the fact that women are human beings, too, as variable as we are. You act on the assumption that they're all the same one— and that one is a completely unearthly being of your own conception. This letter isn't written to Mary Todd—it's written to yourself. Every line of it is intended to provide salve for your own conscience.   ABE (*rising; coldly*)

Do I understand that you will not deliver it for me?

JOSH

No, Abe—I shall not.

ABE (*angrily*)

Then some one else will!

JOSH (*scornfully*)

Yes. You could give it to the minister, to hand to the bride when he arrives for the ceremony. But —I hope, Abe, you won't send it till you're feeling a little calmer in your mind. . . .

ABE (*vehemently, turning to* JOSH)

How can I ever be calm in my mind until this thing is settled, and out of the way, once and for all? Have you got eyes in your head, Josh? Can't you see that I'm desperate?

JOSH

I can see that plainly, Abe. I think your situation is more desperate even than you imagine, and I believe you should have the benefit of some really intelligent medical advice.

ABE (*seating himself at* BILLY's *table*)

The trouble with me isn't anything that a doctor can cure.

JOSH

There's a good man named Dr. Drake, who makes a specialty of treating people who get into a state of mind like yours, Abe . . .

ABE (*utterly miserable*)

So that's how you've figured it! I've done what I've threatened to do many times before: I've gone crazy. Well—you know me better than most men, Josh—and perhaps you're not far off right. I just feel that I've got to the end of my rope, and I must let go, and drop—and where I'll land, I don't know, and whether I'll survive the fall, I don't know that either. . . . But—this I *do* know: I've got to get out of this thing—I can't go through with it—I've got to have my release!

(JOSH *has turned to the window. Suddenly he turns back, toward* ABE.)

JOSH

Ninian Edwards is coming up. Why not show this letter to him and ask for his opinion. . . .

ABE (*interrupting, with desperation*)

No, no! Don't say a word of any of this to him! Put that letter in your pocket. I can't bear to discuss this business with him, now.

(JOSH *puts the letter in his pocket and crosses to the couch.*)

JOSH

Hello, Ninian.

NINIAN (*heartily, from off*)

Hello, Josh! Happy New Year! (NINIAN *comes in. He wears a handsome, fur-trimmed great-coat, and carries two silver-headed canes, one of them in a baize bag, which he lays down on the table at the right.*)

NINIAN

And Happy New Year, Abe—in fact, the happiest of your whole life!

ABE

Thank you, Ninian. And Happy New Year to you.

NINIAN (*opening his coat*)

That didn't sound much as if you meant it. (*He goes to the stove to warm his hands.*) However, you can be forgiven today, Abe. I suppose you're inclined to be just a wee bit nervous. (*He chuckles and winks at* JOSH.) God—but it's cold in here! Don't you ever light this stove?

ABE

The fire's all laid. Go ahead and light it, if you want.

NINIAN (*striking a match*)

You certainly are in one of your less amiable moods today. (*He lights the stove.*)

JOSH

Abe's been feeling a little under the weather.

NINIAN

So it seems. He looks to me as if he'd been to a funeral.

ABE

That's where I have been.

NINIAN (*disbelieving*)

What? A funeral on your wedding day?

JOSH

They buried Abe's oldest friend, Bowling Green, this morning.

NINIAN (*shocked*)

Oh—I'm mighty sorry to hear that, Abe. And— I hope you'll forgive me for—not having known about it.

ABE

Of course, Ninian.

NINIAN

But I'm glad you were there, Abe, at the funeral. It must have been a great comfort to his family.

ABE

I wasn't any comfort to any one. They asked me to deliver an oration, a eulogy of the deceased —and I tried—and I couldn't say a thing. Why do they expect you to strew a lot of flowery phrases over anything so horrible as a dead body? Do they think that Bowling Green's soul needs quotations to give it peace? All that mattered to me was that he was a good, just man—and I loved him —and he's dead.

NINIAN

Why didn't you say that, Abe?

ABE (*rising*)

I told you—they wanted an oration.

NINIAN

Well, Abe—I think Bowling himself would be the first to ask you to put your sadness aside in the prospect of your own happiness, and Mary's— and I'm only sorry that our old friend didn't live to see you two fine people married. (*He is making a gallant attempt to assume a more cheerily nuptial tone.*) I've made all the arrangements with the Reverend Dresser, and Elizabeth is preparing a bang-up dinner—so you can be sure the whole affair will be carried off handsomely *and* painlessly.

(BILLY HERNDON *comes in. He carries a bottle in his coat pocket, and is already more than a little drunk and sullen, but abnormally articulate.*) Ah, Billy—Happy New Year!

BILLY

The same to you, Mr. Edwards. (*He puts the bottle down on the table and takes his coat off.*)

NINIAN

I brought you a wedding present, Abe. Thought you'd like to make a brave show when you first walk out with your bride. It came from the same place in Louisville where I bought mine.

(*He picks up one of the canes and hands it proudly to* ABE, *who takes it and inspects it gravely.*)

ABE

It's very fine, Ninian. And I thank you. (*He takes the cane over to his desk and seats himself.*)

NINIAN

Well—I'll frankly confess that in getting it for
you, I was influenced somewhat by consideration
for Mary and her desire for keeping up appear-
ances. And in that connection—I know you'll forgive me, Josh, and you, too, Billy, if I say something of a somewhat personal nature?

BILLY (*truculent*)

If you want me to leave you, I shall be glad
to. . . .

NINIAN

No, please, Billy—I merely want to speak a word
or two as another of Abe's friends; it's my last
chance before the ceremony. Of course, the fact
that the bride is my sister-in-law gives me a little
added responsibility in wishing to promote the
success of this marriage. (*He crosses to* ABE.)
And a success it will be, Abe . . . if only you will
bear in mind one thing: you must keep a tight rein
on her ambition. My wife tells me that even as a
child, she had delusions of grandeur—she predicted
to one and all that the man she would marry would
be President of the United States. (*He turns to*
JOSH.) You know how it is—every boy in the
country plans some day to be president, and every
little girl plans to marry him. (*Again to* ABE:)
But Mary is one who hasn't entirely lost those
youthful delusions. So I urge you to beware.
Don't let her talk you into any gallant crusades

or wild goose chases. Let her learn to be satisfied
with the estate to which God hath brought her.
With which, I shall conclude my pre-nuptial ser-
mon. (*He buttons his coat.*) I shall see you all at
the house at five o'clock, and I want you to make
sure that Abe is looking his prettiest.

JOSH

Good-bye, Ninian.

(NINIAN *goes out.* ABE *turns again to the desk
and stares at nothing.* BILLY *takes the bottle and
a cup from his desk and pours himself a stiff drink.
He raises the cup toward* ABE.)

BILLY (*huskily*)

Mr. Lincoln, I beg leave to drink to your health
and happiness . . . and to that of the lady who will
become your wife.

(ABE *makes no response.* BILLY *drinks it down,
then puts the cup back on the table.*)

You don't want to accept my toast because you
think it wasn't sincere. And I'll admit I've made
it plain that I've regretted the step you've taken.
I thought that in this marriage, you were lowering
yourself—you were trading your honor for some
exalted family connections. . . . I wish to apologize
for so thinking. . . .

ABE

No apologies required, Billy.

BILLY

I doubt that Miss Todd and I will ever get

along well together. But I'm now convinced that our aims are the same—particularly since I've heard the warnings delivered by her brother-in-law. (*A note of scorn colors his allusion to* NINIAN.) If she really is ambitious for you—if she will never stop driving you, goading you—then I say, God bless her, and give her strength!

(*He has said all this with* ABE's *back to him.* BILLY *pours himself another drink, nearly emptying the large bottle.* ABE *turns and looks at him.*)

ABE

Have you had all of that bottle today?

BILLY

This bottle? Yes—I have.

JOSH

And why not? It's New Year's Day!

BILLY (*looking at* JOSH)

Thank you, Mr. Speed. Thank you for the defense. And I hope you will permit me to propose one more toast. (*He takes a step toward* ABE.) To the President of the United States, and Mrs. Lincoln! (*He drinks.*)

ABE (*grimly*)

I think we can do without any more toasts, Billy.

BILLY

Very well! That's the last one—until after the

wedding. And then, no doubt, the Edwards will serve us with the costliest champagne. And, in case you're apprehensive, I shall be on my best behavior in that distinguished gathering!

ABE

There is not going to be a wedding.

(BILLY *stares at him, and then looks at* JOSH, *and then again at* ABE.)

I have a letter that I want you to deliver to Miss Todd.

BILLY

What letter? What is it?

ABE

Give it to him, Josh.

(JOSH *takes the letter out of his pocket, and puts it in the stove.* ABE *jumps up.*)

You have no right to do that!

JOSH

I know I haven't! But it's done.

(ABE *is staring at* JOSH.)

And don't look at me as if you were planning to break my neck. Of course you could do it, Abe —but you won't. (JOSH *turns to* BILLY.) In that letter, Mr. Lincoln asked Miss Todd for his release. He told her that he had made a mistake in his previous protestations of affection for her, and so he couldn't go through with a marriage which could only lead to endless pain and misery for them both.

ABE (*deeply distressed*)

If that isn't the truth, what is?

JOSH

I'm not disputing the truth of it. I'm only asking you to tell her so, to her face, in the manner of a man.

ABE

It would be a more cruel way. It would hurt her more deeply. For I couldn't help blurting it *all* out—all the terrible things I didn't say in that letter. (*He is speaking with passion.*) I'd have to tell her that I have hatred for her infernal ambition—that I don't want to be ridden and driven, upward and onward through life, with her whip lashing me, and her spurs digging into me! If her poor soul craves importance in life, then let her marry Stephen Douglas. He's ambitious, too. . . . I want only to be left alone! (*He sits down again and leans on the table.*)

JOSH (*bitterly*)

Very well, then—tell her all that! It will be more gracious to admit that you're afraid of her, instead of letting her down flat with the statement that your ardor, such as it was, has cooled.

(BILLY *has been seething with a desire to get into this conversation. Now, with a momentary silence, he plunges.*)

BILLY

May I say something?

ABE

I doubt that you're in much of a condition to contribute. . . .

JOSH

What is it, Billy?

BILLY (*hotly*)

It's just this. Mr. Lincoln, you're not abandoning Miss Mary Todd. No! You're only using her as a living sacrifice, offering her up, in the hope that you will thus gain forgiveness of the gods for your failure to do your own great duty!

ABE (*smoldering*)

Yes! My own great duty. Every one feels called upon to remind me of it, but no one can tell me what it is.

BILLY (*almost tearful*)

I can tell you! I can tell you what is the duty of every man who calls himself an American! It is to perpetuate those truths which were once held to be self-evident: that all men are created equal —that they are endowed with certain inalienable rights—that among these are the right to life, liberty and the pursuit of happiness.

ABE (*angrily*)

And are those rights denied to *me?*

BILLY

Could you ever enjoy them while your mind is full of the awful knowledge that two million of your fellow beings in this country are slaves? Can you take any satisfaction from looking at that flag above your desk, when you know that ten of its stars represent states which are willing to destroy the Union—rather than yield their property rights in the flesh and blood of those slaves? And what of all the States of the future? All the territories of the West—clear out to the Pacific Ocean? Will they be the homes of free men? Are you answering *that* question to your own satisfaction? That is your flag, Mr. Lincoln, and you're proud of it. But what are you doing to save it from being ripped into shreds?

(ABE *jumps to his feet, towers over* BILLY, *and speaks with temper restrained, but with great passion.*)

ABE

I'm minding my own business—that's what I'm doing! And there'd be no threat to the Union if others would do the same. And as to slavery—I'm sick and tired of this righteous talk about it. When you know more about law, you'll know that those property rights you mentioned are guaranteed by the Constitution. And if the Union can't stand on the Constitution, then let it fall!

BILLY

The hell with the Constitution! This is a matter of the rights of living men to freedom—and those came before the Constitution! When the Law denies those rights, then the Law is wrong, and it must be changed, if not by moral protest, then by force! There's no course of action that isn't justified in the defense of freedom! And don't dare to tell me that any one in the world knows that better than you do, Mr. Lincoln. You, who honor the memory of Elijah Lovejoy and every other man who ever died for that very ideal!

ABE (*turning away from him*)

Yes—I honor them—and envy them—because they could believe that their ideals are *worth* dying for. (*He turns to* JOSH *and speaks with infinite weariness.*) All right, Josh—I'll go up now and talk to Mary—and then I'm going away. . . .

JOSH

Where, Abe?

ABE (*dully*)

I don't know.

(*He goes out and closes the door after him. After a moment,* BILLY *rushes to the door, opens it, and shouts after* ABE.)

BILLY

You're quitting, Mr. Lincoln! As surely as there's a God in Heaven, He knows that you're running away from your obligations to Him, and to your fellow-men, and your own immortal soul!

JOSH (*drawing* BILLY *away from the door*)

Billy—Billy—leave him alone. He's a sick man.

BILLY (*sitting down at the table*)

What can we do for him, Mr. Speed? What can we do?

BILLY *is now actually in tears.*)

JOSH

I don't know, Billy. (*He goes to the window and looks out.*) He'll be in such a state of emotional upheaval, he'll want to go away by himself, for a long time. Just as he did after the death of poor little Ann Rutledge. He'll go out and wander on the prairies, trying to grope his way back into the wilderness from which he came. There's nothing we can do for him, Billy. He'll have to do it for himself.

BILLY (*fervently*)

May God be with him!

END OF SCENE VI

SCENE VII

On the prairie, near New Salem. It is a clear, cool, moonlit evening, nearly two years after the preceding scene.

In the foreground is a campfire. Around it are packing cases, blanket rolls and one ancient trunk. In the background is a covered wagon, standing at an angle, so that the opening at the back of it is visible to the audience.

SETH GALE is standing by the fire, holding his seven-year-old son, JIMMY, in his arms. The boy is wrapped up in a blanket.

JIMMY

I don't want to be near the fire, Paw. I'm burning up. Won't you take the blanket offen me, Paw?

SETH

No, son. You're better off if you keep yourself covered.

JIMMY

I want some water, Paw. Can't I have some water?

SETH

Yes! Keep quiet, Jimmy! Gobey's getting the water for you now. (*He looks off to the right, and sees JACK ARMSTRONG coming.*)

Hello, Jack, I was afraid you'd got lost.

JACK (*coming in*)

I couldn't get lost anywhere's around New Salem. How's the boy?

SETH (*with a cautionary look at* JACK)

He—he's a little bit thirsty. Did you find Abe?

JACK

Yes—it took me some time because he'd wandered off—went out to the old cemetery across the river to visit Ann Rutledge's grave.

SETH

Is he coming here?

JACK

He said he'd better go get Doc Chandler who lives on the Winchester Road. He'll be along in a while. (*He comes up to* JIMMY.) How you feelin', Jimmy?

JIMMY

I'm burning . . .
(AGGIE *appears, sees* JACK.)

AGGIE

Oh—I'm glad you're back, Mr. Armstrong.

JACK

There'll be a doctor here soon, Mrs. Gale.

AGGIE

Thank God for that! Bring him into the wagon, Seth. I got a nice, soft bed all ready for him.

SETH

You hear that, Jimmy? Your ma's fixed a place where you can rest comfortable.

(AGGIE *retreats into the wagon.*)

JIMMY

When'll Gobey come back? I'm thirsty. When'll he bring the water?

SETH

Right away, son. You can trust Gobey to get your water. (*He hands* JIMMY *into the wagon.*)

JACK

He's worse, ain't he?

SETH (*in a despairing tone*)

Yes. The fever's been raging something fierce since you left. It'll sure be a relief when Abe gets here. He can always do something to put confidence in you.

JACK

How long since you've seen Abe, Seth?

SETH

Haven't laid eyes on him since I left here—eight —nine years ago. We've corresponded some.

JACK

Well—you may be surprised when you see him. He's changed plenty since he went to Springfield. He climbed up pretty high in the world, but he appears to have slipped down lately. He ain't much like his old comical self.

SETH

Well, I guess we all got to change. (*He starts up, hearing* GOBEY *return.*) Aggie!
(GOBEY, *a Negro, comes in from the left, carrying a bucket of water.* AGGIE *appears from the wagon.*)
Here's Gobey with the water.

GOBEY

Yes, Miss Aggie. Here you are. (*He hands it up.*)

AGGIE

Thanks, Gobey. (*She goes back into the wagon.*)

GOBEY

How's Jimmy now, Mr. Seth?

SETH

About the same.

GOBEY (*shaking his head*)

I'll get some more water for the cooking. (*He picks up a kettle and a pot and goes.*)

SETH (*to* JACK)

It was a bad thing to have happen, all right—the boy getting sick—when we were on an expedition like this. No doctor—no way of caring for him.

JACK

How long you been on the road, Seth?

SETH

More than three months. Had a terrible time in the Pennsylvania Mountains, fearful rains and every stream flooded. I can tell you, there was more than one occasion when I wanted to turn back and give up the whole idea. But—when you get started—you just can't turn . . . (*He is looking off right.*) Say! Is that Abe coming now?

JACK (*rising*)

Yep. That's him.

SETH (*delighted*)

My God, look at him! Store clothes and a plug hat! Hello—Abe!

ABE

Hello, Seth. (*He comes on and shakes hands, warmly*) I'm awful glad to see you again, Seth.

SETH

And me, too, Abe.

ABE

It did my heart good when I heard you were on your way West. Where's your boy?

SETH

He's in there—in the wagon. . . .
(AGGIE *has appeared from the wagon.*)

AGGIE

Is that the doctor?

SETH

No, Aggie—this is the man I was telling you about I wanted so much to see. This is Mr. Abe Lincoln—my wife, Mrs. Gale.

ABE

Pleased to meet you, Mrs. Gale.

AGGIE

Pleased to meet you, Mr. Lincoln.

ABE

Doc Chandler wasn't home. They said he was expected over at the Boger farm at midnight. I'll go there then and fetch him.

SETH

It'll be a friendly act, Abe.

AGGIE

We'll be in your debt, Mr. Lincoln.

ABE

In the meantime, Mrs. Gale, I'd like to do whatever I can. . . .

SETH

There's nothing to do, Abe. The boy's got the swamp fever, and we're just trying to keep him quiet.

AGGIE (*desperately*)

There's just one thing I would wish—is—is there any kind of a preacher around this God-forsaken place?

SETH (*worried*)

Preacher?

ABE

Do you know of any, Jack?

JACK

No. There ain't a preacher within twenty miles of New Salem now.

AGGIE

Well—I only thought if there was, we might get him here to say a prayer for Jimmy.

(*She goes back into the wagon.* SETH *looks after her with great alarm.*)

SETH

She wants a preacher. That looks as if she'd given up, don't it?

JACK

It'd probably just comfort her.

ABE

Is your boy very sick, Seth?

SETH

Yes—he is.

JACK

Why don't *you* speak a prayer, Abe? You could always think of somethin' to say.

ABE

I'm afraid I'm not much of a hand at praying. I couldn't think of a blessed thing that would be of any comfort.

SETH

Never mind. It's just a—a religious idea of Aggie's. Sit down, Abe.

ABE (*looking at the wagon*)

So you've got your dream at last, Seth. You're doing what you and I used to talk about—you're moving.

SETH

Yes, Abe. We got crowded out of Maryland. The city grew up right over our farm. So—we're headed for a place where there's more room. I wrote you —about four months back—to tell you we were starting out, and I'd like to meet up with you here. I thought it was just possible you might consider joining in this trip.

ABE

It took a long time for your letter to catch up with me, Seth. I've just been drifting—down around Indiana and Kentucky where I used to live. (*He sits down on a box.*) Do you aim to settle in Nebraska?

SETH

No, we're not going to stop there. We're going right across the continent—all the way to Oregon.

ABE (*deeply impressed*)

Oregon?

JACK

Sure. That's where they're all headin' for now.

SETH

We're making first for a place called Westport Landing—that's in Kansas right on the frontier—where they outfit the wagon trains for the far West. You join up there with a lot of others who are like-minded, so you've got company when you're crossing the plains and the mountains.

ABE

It's staggering—to think of the distance you're going. And you'll be taking the frontier along with you.

SETH

It may seem like a fool-hardy thing to do—but we heard too many tales of the black earth out there, and the balance of rainfall and sunshine.

JACK

Why don't you go with them, Abe? That country out west is gettin' settled fast. Why—last week alone, I counted more than two hundred wagons went past here—people from all over—Pennsylvania, Connecticut, Vermont—all full of jubilation at the notion of gettin' land. By God, I'm goin' too, soon as I can get me a wagon. They'll need men like me to fight the Indians for 'em—and they'll need men with brains, like you, Abe, to tell 'em how to keep the peace.

ABE (*looking off*)

It's a temptation to go, I can't deny that.

JACK

Then what's stoppin' you from doin' it? You said yourself you've just been driftin'.

ABE

Maybe that's it—maybe I've been drifting too long. . . . (*He changes the subject.*) Is it just the three of you, Seth?

SETH

That's all. The three of us and Gobey, the nigger.

ABE

Is he your slave?

SETH

Gobey? Hell, no! He's a free man! My father freed his father twenty years ago. But we've had to be mighty careful about Gobey. You see, where we come from, folks are pretty uncertain how they feel about the slave question, and lots of good free niggers get snaked over the line into Virginia and then sold down river before you know it. And when you try to go to court and assert their legal rights, you're beaten at every turn by the damned, dirty shyster lawyers. That's why we've been keeping well up in free territory on this trip.

ABE

Do you think it will be free in Oregon?

SETH

Of course it will! It's go to——

ABE (*bitterly*)

Oh no, it hasn't, Seth. Not with the politicians in Washington selling out the whole West piece by piece to the slave traders.

SETH (*vehemently*)

That territory has got to be free! If this country ain't strong enough to protect its citizens from slavery, then we'll cut loose from it and join with Canada. Or, better yet, we'll make a *new* country out there in the far west.

ABE (*gravely*)

A new country?

SETH

Why not?

ABE

I was just thinking—old Mentor Graham once said to me that some day the United States might be divided up into many hostile countries, like Europe.

SETH

Well—let it be! Understand—I love this country and I'd fight for it. And I guess George Washington and the rest of them loved England and fought for it when they were young—but they didn't hesitate to cut loose when the government failed to play fair and square with 'em. . .

JACK

By God, if Andy Jackson was back in the White House, he'd run out them traitors with a horse-whip!

ABE

It'd be a bad day for us Americans, Seth, if we lost you, and your wife, and your son.

SETH (*breaking*)

My son!—Oh—I've been talking big—but it's empty talk. If he dies—there won't be enough spirit left in us to push on any further. What's the use of working for a future when you know there won't be anybody growing up to enjoy it. Excuse me, Abe —but I'm feeling pretty scared.

ABE (*suddenly rises*)

You mustn't be scared, Seth. I know I'm a poor one to be telling you that—because I've been scared all my life. But—seeing you now—and thinking of the big thing you've set out to do—well, it's made me feel pretty small. It's made me feel that I've got to do something, too, to keep you and your kind in the United States of America. You mustn't quit, Seth! Don't let anything beat you—don't you ever give up!

(AGGIE *comes out of the wagon. She is very frightened.*)

AGGIE

Seth!

SETH

What is it, Aggie?

AGGIE

He's worse, Seth! He'd moaning in his sleep, and he's grosping for breath. . . .

(*She is crying.* SETH *takes her in his arms.*)

SETH

Never mind, honey. Never mind. When the doctor gets here, he'll fix him up in no time. It's all right, honey. He'll get well.

ABE

If you wish me to, Mrs. Gale—I'll try to speak a prayer.

(*They look at him.*)

JACK

That's the way to talk, Abe!

SETH

We'd be grateful for anything you might say, Abe.

(ABE *takes his hat off. As he starts speaking,* GOBEY *comes in from the left and stops reverently to listen.*)

ABE

Oh God, the father of all living, I ask you to look with gentle mercy upon this little boy who is here, lying sick in this covered wagon. His people are travelling far, to seek a new home in the wilderness, to do your work, God, to make this earth a good place for your children to live in. They can see clearly where they're going, and they're not afraid to face all the perils that lie along the way. I humbly beg you not to take their child from them. Grant him the freedom of life. Do not condemn him to the imprisonment of death. Do not deny him his birthright. Let him know the sight of great plains and high mountains, of green valleys and wide rivers. For this little boy is an American, and these things belong to him, and he to them. Spare him, that he too may strive for the ideal for which his fathers have labored, so faithfully and for so long. Spare him and give him his fathers' strength—give us all strength. Oh God, to do the work that is before us. I ask you this favor, in the name of *your* son, Jesus Christ, who died upon the Cross to set men free. Amen.

GOBEY (*with fervor*)

Amen!

SETH AND AGGIE (*murmuring*)

Amen!

(ABE *puts his hat on.*)

ABE

It's getting near midnight. I'll go over to the Boger farm and get the doctor. (*He goes out.*)

SETH

Thank you, Abe.

AGGIE

Thank you—thank you, Mr. Lincoln.

GOBEY

God bless you, Mr. Lincoln!
(*The lights fade quickly.*)

END OF SCENE VII

SCENE VIII

Again the parlor of the Edwards house. A few days after preceding scene.

MARY *is seated, reading a book.*

After a moment, the MAID *enters.*

MAID

Miss Mary—Mr. Lincoln is here.

MARY

Mr. Lincoln! (*She sits still a moment in an effort to control her emotions, then sharply closes the book and rises.*)

MAID

Will you see him, Miss Mary?

MARY

Yes—in one moment.

(*The* MAID *goes off.* MARY *turns, drops her book on the sofa, then moves over toward the right, struggling desperately to compose herself. At the fireplace, she stops and turns to face* ABE *as he enters.*)
I'm glad to see you again, Mr. Lincoln.

(*There is considerable constraint between them. He is grimly determined to come to the point with the fewest possible words; she is making a gallant, well-bred attempt to observe the social amenities.*)

ABE

Thank you, Mary. You may well wonder why I have thrust myself on your mercy in this manner.

MARY (*quickly*)

I'm sure you're always welcome in Ninian's house.

ABE

After my behavior at our last meeting here, I have not been welcome company for myself.

MARY

You've been through a severe illness. Joshua Speed has kept us informed of it. We've been greatly concerned.

ABE

It is most kind of you.

MARY

But you're restored to health now—you'll return to your work, and no doubt you'll be running for the assembly again—or perhaps you have larger plans?

ABE

I have no plans, Mary. (*He seems to brace himself.*) But I wish to tell you that I am sorry for the things that I said on that unhappy occasion which was to have been our wedding day.

MARY

You need not say anything about that, Mr. Lincoln. Whatever happened then, it was my own fault.

ABE (*disturbed by this unforeseen avowal*)
Your fault! It was my miserable cowardice——

MARY

I was blinded by my own self-confidence! I—I loved you. (*For a moment her firm voice falters, but she immediately masters that tendency toward weakness.*) And I believed I could make you love me. I believed we might achieve a real communion of spirit, and the fire of my determination would burn in you. You would become a man and a leader of men! But you didn't wish that. (*She turns away.*) I knew you had strength—but I did not know you would use it, all of it, to resist your own magnificent destiny.

ABE (*deliberately*)

It is true, Mary—you once had faith in me which I was far from deserving. But the time has come, at last, when I wish to strive to deserve it.
(MARY *looks at him, sharply.*)
When I behaved in that shameful manner toward you, I did so because I thought that our ways were separate and could never be otherwise. I've come to the conclusion that I was wrong. I believe that our destinies are together, for better or for worse, and I again presume to ask you to be my wife. I fully realize, Mary, that taking me back now would involve humiliation for you.

MARY (*flaring*)

I am not afraid of humiliation, if I know it will be wiped out by ultimate triumph! But there can be no triumph unless you yourself are sure. What was it that brought you to this change of heart and mind?

ABE

On the prairie, I met an old friend of mine who was moving West, with his wife and child, in a covered wagon. He asked me to go with him, and I was strongly tempted to do so. (*There is great sadness in his tone—but he seems to collect himself, and turns to her again, speaking with a sort of resignation.*) But then I knew that was not my direction. The way I must go is the way you have always wanted me to go.

MARY

And you will promise that never again will you falter, or turn to run away?

ABE

I promise, Mary—if you will have me—I shall devote myself for the rest of my days to trying—to do what is right—as God gives me power to see what is right.

(*She looks at him, trying to search him. She would like to torment him, for a while, with artful indecision. But she can not do it.*)

MARY

Very well then—I shall be your wife. I shall fight

by your side—till death do us part. *She runs to him and clutches him.*) Abe! I love you—oh, I love you! Whatever becomes of the two of us, I'll die loving you! (*She is sobbing wildly on his shoulder. Awkwardly, he lifts his hands and takes hold of her in a loose embrace. He is staring down at the carpet, over her shoulder.*)

CURTAIN

END OF ACT II

ACT III

ACT III

SCENE IX

A speakers' platform in an Illinois town. It is a summer evening in the year 1858.

A light shines down on the speaker at the front of the platform.

At the back of the platform are three chairs. At the right sits JUDGE STEPHEN A. DOUGLAS—*at the left,* ABE, *who has his plug hat on and makes occasional notes on a piece of paper on his knee. The chair in the middle is for* NINIAN, *acting as Moderator, who is now at the front of the platform.*

NINIAN

We have now heard the leading arguments from the two candidates for the high office of United States Senator from Illinois—Judge Stephen A. Douglas and Mr. Abraham Lincoln. A series of debates between these two eminent citizens of Illinois has focussed upon our state the attention of the entire nation, for here are being discussed the vital issues which now affect the lives of all Americans and the whole future history of our beloved country. According to the usual custom of debate, each of the candidates will now speak in rebuttal. . . . Judge Douglas.

(NINIAN *retires and sits, as* DOUGLAS *comes forward. He is a brief but magnetic man, confident of his powers.*)

DOUGLAS

My fellow citizens: My good friend, Mr. Lincoln, has addressed you with his usual artless sincerity, his pure, homely charm, his perennial native humor. He has even devoted a generously large portion of his address to most amiable remarks upon my fine qualities as a man, if not as a statesman. For which I express deepest gratitude. But—at the same time—I most earnestly beg you not to be deceived by his seeming innocence, his carefully cultivated spirit of good will. For in each of his little homilies lurk concealed weapons. Like Brutus, in Shakespeare's immortal tragedy, Mr. Lincoln is an honorable man. But, also like Brutus, he is an adept at the art of inserting daggers between an opponent's ribs, just when said opponent least expects it. Behold me, gentlemen—I am covered with scars. And yet—somehow or other—I am still upright. Perhaps because I am supported by that sturdy prop called "Truth." Truth—which, crushed to earth by the assassin's blades, doth rise again! Mr. Lincoln makes you laugh with his pungent anecdotes. Then he draws tears from your eyes with his dramatic pictures of the plight of the black slave labor in the South. Always, he guides you skilfully to the threshold of truth, but then, as you are about to cross it, diverts your attention elsewhere. For one thing—he never, by any mischance, makes reference to the condition of labor here in the North! Oh, no! Perhaps New England is so far beyond the bounds of his parochial ken that he does not know that tens of thousands of working men and women in the textile industry are now on STRIKE! And why are they on strike? Because from early morning to dark of night— fourteen hours a day—those "free" citizens must toil at shattering looms in soulless factories and never see the sun; and then, when their fearful day's work at last comes to its exhausted end, these ill-clad and undernourished laborers must trudge home to their foul abodes in tenements that are not fit habitations for rats! What kind of Liberty is this? And if Mr. Lincoln has not heard of conditions in Massachusetts—how has it escaped his attention that here in our own great state no wheels are now turning on that mighty railroad, the Illinois Central? Because its oppressed workers are also on STRIKE! Because they too demand a living wage! So it is throughout the North. Hungry men, marching through the streets in ragged order, promoting riots, because they are not paid enough to keep the flesh upon the bones of their babies! What kind of Liberty is *this*? And what kind of equality? Mr. Lincoln harps constantly on this subject of equality. He repeats over and over the argument used by Lovejoy and other abolitionists: to wit, that the Declaration of Independence having declared all men free and equal, by divine law, thus Negro equality is an inalienable right. Contrary to this absurd assumption stands the verdict of the Supreme Court, as it was clearly stated by Chief Justice Taney in the case of Dred Scott. The Negroes are established by this decision as an inferior race of beings, subjugated by the dominant race, enslaved and, therefore, *property*—like all other property! But Mr. Lincoln is inclined to dispute the constitutional authority of the Supreme Court. He has implied, if he did not say so outright, that the Dred Scott decision was a prejudiced one, which must be over-ruled by the voice of the people. Mr. Lincoln is a lawyer, and I presume, therefore, that he knows that when he seeks to destroy public confidence in the integrity, the inviolability of the Supreme Court, he is preaching *revolution!* He is attempting to stir up odium and rebellion in this country against the constituted authorities; he is stimulating the passions of men to resort to violence and to mobs, instead of to the law. He is setting brother against brother! There can be but one consequence of such inflammatory persuasion—and that is *Civil War!* He asks me to state my opinion of the Dred Scott Decision, and I answer him unequivocally by saying, "I take the decisions of the Supreme Court as the law of the land, and I intend to obey them as such!" Nor will I be swayed from that position by all the rantings of all the fanatics who preach "racial equality," who ask us to vote, and eat, and sleep, and marry with Negroes! And I say further—Let each State mind its own business and leave its neighbors alone. If we will stand by that principle, then Mr. Lincoln will find that this great republic can exist forever divided into free and slave states. We can go on as we have done, increasing in wealth, in population, in power, until we shall be the admiration and the terror of the world! (*He glares at the audience, then turns, mopping his brow, and resumes his seat.*)

NINIAN (*rising*)

Mr. Lincoln.

(*ABE glances at his notes, takes his hat off, puts the notes in it, then rises slowly and comes forward. He speaks quietly, reasonably. His words come from an emotion so profound that it needs no advertisement.*)

ABE

Judge Douglas has paid tribute to my skill with the dagger. I thank him for that, but I must also admit that he can do more with that weapon than I can. He can keep ten daggers flashing in the air at one time. Fortunately, he's so good at it that none of the knives ever falls and hurts anybody. The Judge can condone slavery in the South and protest hotly against its extension to the North.

He can crowd loyalty to the Union and defense of
states' sovereignty into the same breath. Which
reminds me—and I hope the Judge will allow me one
more homely little anecdote, because I'd like to tell
about a woman down in Kentucky. She came out
of her cabin one day and found her husband grap-
pling with a ferocious bear. It was a fight to the
death, and the bear was winning. The struggling
husband called to his wife, "For heaven's sake, *help*
me!" The wife asked what could *she* do? Said the
husband, "You could at least *say* something en-
couraging." But the wife didn't want to seem to be
taking sides in this combat, so she just hollered,
"Go it husband—go it bear!" Now, you heard the
Judge make allusion to those who advocate voting
and eating and marrying and sleeping with Negroes. Whether he meant me specifically, I do not
know. If he did, I can say that just because I do
not want a colored woman for a slave, I don't necessarily want her for a wife. I need not have her for
either. I can just leave her alone. In some respects,
she certainly is not my equal, any more than I am
the Judge's equal, in some respects; but in her natural right to eat the bread she earns with her own
hands without asking leave of some one else, she is
my equal, and the equal of all others. And as to
sleeping with Negroes—the Judge may be interested
to know that the slave states have produced more
than four hundred thousand mulattoes—and I don't
think many of them are the children of abolitionists.

That word "abolitionists" brings to mind New England, which also has been mentioned. I assure Judge Douglas that I have been there, and I have seen those cheerless brick prisons called factories, and the workers trudging silently home through the darkness. In those factories, cotton that was picked by black slaves is woven into cloth by white people who are separated from slavery by no more than fifty cents a day. As an American, I cannot be proud that such conditions exist. But —as an American—I can ask: would any of those striking workers in the North elect to change places with the slaves in the South? Will they not rather say, "The remedy is in *our* hands!" And, still as an American, I can say—thank God we live under a system by which men have the *right* to strike! I am not preaching rebellion. I don't have to. This country, with its institutions, belongs to the people who inhabit it. Whenever they shall grow weary of the existing government, they can exercise their constitutional right of amending it, or their revolutionary right to dismember or overthrow it. If the founding fathers gave us anything, they gave us that. And I am not preaching disrespect for the Supreme Court. I am only saying that the decisions of mortal men are often influenced by unjudicial bias—and the Supreme Court is composed of mortal men, most of whom, it so happens, come from the privileged class in the South. There is an old saying that judges are just as honest as other men, and not more so; and in case some of you are wondering who said that, it was Thomas Jefferson. (*He has half turned to* DOUGLAS.) The purpose of the Dred Scott Decision is to make property, and nothing but property, of the Negro in all states of the Union. It is the old issue of property rights versus human rights—an issue that will continue in this country when these poor tongues of Judge Douglas and myself shall long have been silent. It is the eternal struggle between two principles. The one is the common right of humanity, and the other the divine right of kings. It is the same spirit that says, "You toil and work and earn bread, and I'll eat it." Whether those words come from the mouth of a king who bestrides his people and lives by the fruit of their labor, or from one race of men who seek to enslave another race, it is the same tyrannical principle. As a nation, we began by declaring, "All men are created equal." There was no mention of any exceptions to the rule in the Declaration of Independence. But we now practically read it, "All men are created equal except Negroes." If we accept this doctrine of race or class discrimination, what is to stop us from decreeing in the future that "All men are created equal except Negroes, foreigners, Catholics, Jews, or—just poor people?" That is the conclusion toward which the advocates of slavery are driving us. Many good citizens, North and South, agree with the Judge that we should accept

that conclusion—don't stir up trouble—"Let each
State mind its own business." That's the safer
course, for the time being. But—I advise you to
watch out! When you have enslaved any of your
fellow beings, dehumanized him, denied him all
claim to the dignity of manhood, placed him among
the beasts, among the damned, are you quite sure
that the demon you have thus created, will not turn
and rend *you?* When you begin qualifying freedom, watch out for the consequences to *you!* And
I am not preaching civil war. All I am trying to
do—now, and as long as I live—is to state and re-
state the fundamental virtues of our democracy,
which have made us great, and which can make us
greater. I believe most seriously that the perpetu-
ation of those virtues is now endangered, not only
by the honest proponents of slavery, but even more
by those who echo Judge Douglas in shouting,
"Leave it alone!" This is the complacent policy
of indifference to evil, and that policy I cannot
but hate. I hate it because of the monstrous injustice of slavery itself. I hate it because it de-
prives our republic of its just influence in the
world; enables the enemies of free institutions
everywhere to taunt us as hypocrites; causes the
real friends of freedom to doubt our sincerity; and
especially because it forces so many good men
among ourselves into an open war with the very
fundamentals of civil liberty, denying the good
faith of the Declaration of Independence, and in-

sisting that there is no right principle of action but *self-interest*. . . . In his final words tonight, the Judge said that we may be "the terror of the world." I don't think we want to be that. I think we would prefer to be the encouragement of the world, the proof that man is at last worthy to be free. But—we shall provide no such encouragement, unless we can establish our ability as a nation to live and grow. And we shall surely do neither if these states fail to remain *united*. There can be no distinction in the definitions of liberty as between one section and another, one race and another, one class and another. "A house divided against itself cannot stand." This government can not endure permanently, half slave and half free! (*He turns and goes back to his seat.*)

(*The lights fade.*)

END OF SCENE IX

SCENE X

Parlor of the Edwards home, now being used by the Lincolns. Afternoon of a day in the early Spring of 1860.

Abe is sitting on the couch at the right, with his seven-year-old son, Tad, on his lap. Sitting beside them is another son, Willie, aged nine. The eldest son, Robert, a young Harvard student of seventeen, is sitting by the window, importantly smoking a pipe and listening to the story Abe has been telling the children. Joshua Speed is sitting at the left.

ABE

You must remember, Tad, the roads weren't much good then—mostly nothing more than trails—and it was hard to find my way in the darkness. . . .

WILLIE

Were you scared?

ABE

Yes—I was scared.

WILLIE

Of Indians?

ABE

No—there weren't any of them left around here. I was afraid I'd get lost, and the boy would die, and it would be all my fault. But, finally, I found

141

the doctor. He was very tired, and wanted to go to bed, and he grumbled a lot, but I made him come along with me then and there.

WILLIE

Was the boy dead?

ABE

No, Willie. He wasn't dead. But he was pretty sick. The doctor gave him a lot of medicine.

TAD

Did it taste bad, Pa?

ABE

I presume it did. But it worked. I never saw those nice people again, but I've heard from them every so often. That little boy was your age, Tad, but now he's a grown man with a son almost as big as you are. He lives on a great big farm, in a valley with a river that runs right down from the tops of the snow mountains. . . .

(MARY *comes in.*)

MARY

Robert! You are smoking in my parlor!

ROBERT (*wearily*)

Yes, Mother. (*He rises.*)

MARY

I have told you that I shall not tolerate tobacco smoke in my parlor or, indeed, in any part of my house, and I mean to . . .

ABE

Come, come, Mary—you must be respectful to
a Harvard man. Take it out to the woodshed,
Bob.

ROBERT

Yes, Father.

MARY

And this will not happen again!

ROBERT

No, Mother. (*He goes out.*)

ABE

I was telling the boys a story about some pioneers I knew once.

MARY

It's time for you children to make ready for
your supper.

(*The* CHILDREN *promptly get up to go.*)

WILLIE

But what happened after that, Pa?

ABE

Nothing. Everybody lived happily ever after.
Now run along.

(WILLIE *and* TAD *run out.*)

JOSH

What time *is* it, Mary?

MARY

It's nearly half past four. (*She is shaking the smoke out of the curtains.*)

JOSH

Half past four, Abe. Those men will be here any minute.

ABE (*rising*)

Good Lord!

MARY (*turning sharply to* ABE)

What men?

ABE

Some men from the East. One of them's a political leader named Crimmin—and there's a Mr. Sturveson—he's a manufacturer—and . . .

MARY (*impressed*)

Henry D. Sturveson?

ABE

That's the one—and also the Reverend Dr. Barrick from Boston.

MARY (*sharply*)

What are they coming here for?

ABE

I don't precisely know—but I suspect that it's to see if I'm fit to be a candidate for President of the United States.

(MARY *is, for the moment, speechless.*)

I suppose they want to find out if we still live in a log cabin and keep pigs under the bed. . . .

MARY (*in a fury*)

And you didn't *tell* me!

ABE

I'm sorry, Mary—the matter just slipped my . . .

MARY

You forgot to tell me that we're having the most important guests who ever crossed the threshold of my house!

ABE

They're not guests. They're only here on business.

MARY (*bitterly*)

Yes! Rather important business, it seems to me. They want to see us as we *are*—crude, sloppy, vulgar Western barbarians, living in a house that reeks of foul tobacco smoke.

ABE

We can explain about having a son at Harvard.

MARY

If I'd only *known!* If you had only given me a little time to prepare for them. Why didn't you put on your best suit? And those filthy old boots!

ABE

Well, Mary, I clean forgot. . . .

MARY

I declare, Abraham Lincoln, I believe you would have treated me with much more consideration if I had been your slave, instead of your wife! You have never, for one moment, stopped to think that perhaps I have some interests, some concerns, in the life we lead together. . . .

ABE

I'll try to clean up my boots a little, Mary.
(*He goes out, glad to escape from this painful scene.* MARY *looks after him. Her lip is quivering. She wants to avoid tears.*)

MARY (*seating herself; bitterly*)

You've seen it all, Joshua Speed. Every bit of it—courtship, if you could call it that, change of heart, change back again, and marriage, eighteen years of it. And you probably think just as all the others do—that I'm a bitter, nagging woman, and I've tried to kill his spirit, and drag him down to my level. . . .

(JOSH *rises and goes over to her.*)

JOSH (*quietly*)

No, Mary. I think no such thing. Remember, I know Abe, too.

MARY

There never could have been another man such as he is! I've read about many that have gone up in the world, and all of them seemed to have to fight to assert themselves every inch of the way, against the opposition of their enemies and the lack of understanding in their own friends. But he's never had any of that. He's never had an enemy, and every one of his friends has always been completely confident in him. Even before I met him, I was told that he had a glorious future, and after I'd known him a day, I was sure of it myself. But he didn't believe it—or, if he did, secretly, he was so afraid of the prospect that he did all in his power to avoid it. He had some poem in his mind, about a life of woe, along a rugged path, that leads to some future doom, and it has been an obsession with him. All these years, I've tried and tried to stir him out of it, but all my efforts have been like so many puny waves, dashing against the Rock of Ages. And now, opportunity, the greatest opportunity, is coming here, to him, right into his own house. And what can I do about it? He *must* take it! He *must* see that this is what he was meant for! But I can't persuade him of it! I'm tired— I'm tired to death! (*The tears now come.*) I thought I could help to shape him, as I knew he should be, and I've succeeded in nothing—but in breaking myself. . . . (*She sobs bitterly.*)

(JOSH *sits down beside her and pats her hand.*)

JOSH (*tenderly*)

I know, Mary. But—there's no reason in heaven and earth for you to reproach yourself. Whatever becomes of Abe Lincoln is in the hands of a God who controls the destinies of all of us, including lunatics, and saints.

(ABE *comes back.*)

ABE (*looking down at his boots*)

I think they look all right now, Mary. (*He looks at* MARY, *who is now trying hard to control her emotion.*)

MARY

You can receive the gentlemen in here. I'll try to prepare some refreshment for them in the dining-room.

(*She goes out.* ABE *looks after her, miserably. There are a few moments of silence. At length,* ABE *speaks, in an off-hand manner.*)

ABE

I presume these men *are* pretty influential.

JOSH

They'll have quite a say in the delegations of three states that may swing the nomination away from Seward.

ABE

Suppose, by some miracle, or fluke, they did nominate me; do you think I'd stand a chance of winning the election?

JOSH

An excellent chance, in my opinion. There'll be four candidates in the field, bumping each other, and opening up the track for a dark horse.

ABE

But the dark horse might run in the wrong direction.

JOSH

Yes—you can always do that, Abe. I know *I* wouldn't care to bet two cents on you.

ABE (*grinning*)

It seems funny to be comparing it to a horse-race, with an old, spavined hack like me. But I've had some mighty energetic jockeys—Mentor Graham, Bowling Green, Bill Herndon, you, and Mary —most of all, Mary.

JOSH (*looking at* ABE)

They don't count now, Abe. You threw 'em all, long ago. When you finally found yourself running against poor little Douglas, you got the bit between your teeth and went like greased lightning. You'd do the same thing to him again, if you could only decide to get started, which you probably won't . . . (*The doorbell jangles.* JOSH *gets up.*)

ABE

I expect that's them now.

JOSH

I'll go see if I can help Mary. (*He starts for the door but turns and looks at* ABE, *and speaks quietly.*) I'd just like to remind you, Abe—there are pretty nearly thirty million people in this country; most of 'em are common people, like you. They're in serious trouble, and they need somebody who understands 'em, as you do. So—when these gentlemen come in—try to be a *little* bit polite to them. (ABE *grins.* JOSH *looks off.*) However— you won't listen to any advice from me.

(JOSH *goes. The door is opened by a* MAID *and* STURVESON, BARRICK, *and* CRIMMIN *come in.* STURVESON *is elderly, wealthy and bland.* BAR— RICK *is a soft Episcopalian dignitary.* CRIMMIN *is a shrewd, humorous fixer.*)

ABE

Come right in, gentlemen. Glad to see you again, Mr. Crimmin.

(*They shake hands.*)

CRIMMIN

How de do, Mr. Lincoln. This is Dr. Barrick of Boston, and Mr. Sturveson, of Philadelphia.

DR. BARRICK

Mr. Lincoln.

STURVESON

I'm honored, Mr. Lincoln.

LINCOLN

Thank you, sir. Pray sit down, gentlemen.

STURVESON

Thank you.

(*They sit.*)

CRIMMIN

Will Mrs. Lincoln seriously object if I light a seegar?

LINCOLN

Go right ahead! I regret that Mrs. Lincoln is not here to receive you, but she will join us presently. (*He sits down.*)

BARRICK (*with great benignity*)

I am particularly anxious to meet Mrs. Lincoln, for I believe, with Mr. Longfellow, that 'as unto the bow the cord is, so unto the man is woman.'

STURVESON (*very graciously*)

And we are here dealing with a bow that is stout indeed.

(ABE *bows slightly in acknowledgment of the compliment.*)

And one with a reputation for shooting straight. So you'll forgive us, Mr. Lincoln, for coming directly to the point.

ABE

Yes, sir. I understand that you wish to inspect the prairie politician in his native lair, and here I am.

STURVESON

It is no secret that we are desperately in need of a candidate—one who is sound, conservative, safe—and clever enough to skate over the thin ice of the forthcoming campaign. Your friends—and there's an increasingly large number of them throughout the country—believe that you are the man.

ABE

Well, Mr. Sturveson, I can tell you that when first I was considered for political office—that was in New Salem, twenty-five years ago—I assured my sponsors of my conservatism. I have subsequently proved it, by never progressing anywhere.

BARRICK (*smiling*)

Then you agree that you are the man we want?

ABE

I'm afraid I can't go quite that far in self-esteem, Dr. Barrick, especially when you have available a statesman and gentleman as eminent as Mr. Seward who, I believe, is both ready and willing.

STURVESON

That's as may be. But please understand that this is not an inquisition. We merely wish to know you better, to gain a clearer idea of your theories on economics, religion and national affairs, in general. To begin with—in one of your memorable debates with Senator Douglas, your opponent indulged in some of his usual demagoguery about industrial conditions in the North, and you replied shrewdly that whereas the slaves in the South . . .

ABE

Yes, I remember the occasion. I replied that I

was thankful that laborers in free states have the right to strike. But that wasn't shrewdness, Mr. Sturveson. It was just the truth.

STURVESON

It has gained for you substantial support from the laboring classes, which is all to the good. But it has also caused a certain amount of alarm among business men, like myself.

ABE

I cannot enlarge on the subject. It seems obvious to me that this nation was founded on the supposition that men have the right to protest, violently if need be, against authority that is unjust or oppressive. (*He turns to* BARRICK.) The Boston Tea Party was a kind of strike. So was the Revolution itself. (*Again to* STURVESON.) So was Nicholas Biddle's attempt to organize the banks against the Jackson administration.

STURVESON

Which is all perfectly true—but—the days of anarchy are over. We face an unprecedented era of industrial expansion—mass production of every conceivable kind of goods—railroads and telegraph lines across the continent—all promoted and developed by private enterprise. In this great work, we must have a free hand, and a firm one, Mr. Lincoln. To put it bluntly, would you, if elected, place the interests of labor above those of capital?

ABE

I cannot answer that, bluntly, or any other way; because I cannot tell what I should do, if elected.

STURVESON

But you must have inclinations toward one side or the other. . . .

ABE

I think you know, Mr. Sturveson, that I am opposed to slavery.

BARRICK

And we of New England applaud your sentiments! We deplore the inhumanity of our Southern friends in . . .

ABE (*to* BARRICK)

There are more forms of slavery than that which is inflicted upon the Negroes in the South. I am opposed to all of them. (*He turns again to* STURVESON.) I believe in our democratic system—the just and generous system which opens the way to all—gives hope to all, and consequent energy and progress and improvement of condition to all, including employer and employee alike.

BARRICK

We support your purpose, Mr. Lincoln, in steadfactly proclaiming the rights of men to resist unjust authority. But I am most anxious to know whether you admit One Authority to whom devotion is unquestioned?

ABE

I presume you refer to the Almighty?

BARRICK

I do.

ABE

I think there has never been any doubt of my submission to His will.

BARRICK

I'm afraid there is a great deal of doubt as to your devotion to His church.

ABE

I realize that, Doctor. They say I'm an atheist, because I've always refused to become a church member.

BARRICK

What have been the grounds of your refusal?

ABE

I have found no churches suitable for my own form of worship. I could not give assent without mental reservations to the long, complicated statements of Christian doctrine which characterize their Articles of Belief and Confessions of Faith. But I can promise you, Dr. Barrick—I shall gladly join any church at any time if its sole qualification for membership is obedience to the Saviour's state-

ment of Law and Gospel: 'Thou shalt love the
Lord thy God with all thy heart and with all thy
soul and with all thy mind, and thou shalt love
thy neighbor as thyself.' . . . But—I beg you gentlemen to excuse me for a moment. I believe Mrs.
Lincoln is preparing a slight collation, and I must
see if I can help with it. . . .

CRIMMIN

Certainly, Mr. Lincoln.

(ABE *goes, closing the door behind him.* CRIM-
MIN *looks at the door, then turns to the others.*)
Well?

BARRICK

The man is unquestionably an infidel. An ideal-
ist—in his curious, primitive way—but an infidel!

STURVESON

And a radical!

CRIMMIN

A radical? Forgive me, gentlemen, if I enjoy
a quiet laugh at that.

STURVESON

Go ahead and enjoy yourself, Crimmin—but I
did not like the way he evaded my direct question.
I tell you, he's as unscrupulous a demagogue as
Douglas. He's a rabble rouser!

CRIMMIN

Of course he is! As a dealer in humbug, he puts
Barnum himself to shame.

STURVESON

Quite possibly—but he is not *safe!*

CRIMMIN

Not safe, eh? And what do you mean by that?

STURVESON

Just what I say. A man who devotes himself so whole-heartedly to currying favor with the mob develops the mob mentality. He becomes a preacher of discontent, of mass unrest. . . .

CRIMMIN

And what about Seward? If we put him up, he'll start right in demanding liberation of the slaves —and then there *will* be discontent and unrest! I ask you to believe me when I tell you that this Lincoln *is* safe—in economics and theology and everything else. After all—what is the essential qualification that we demand of the candidate of our party? It is simply this: that he be able to get himself elected! And there is the man who can do that. (*He points off-stage.*)

STURVESON (*smiling*)

I should like to believe you!

BARRICK

So say we all of us!

CRIMMIN

Then just keep faith in the eternal stupidity of the voters, which is what *he* will appeal to. In that uncouth rail splitter you may observe one of the smoothest, slickest politicians that ever hoodwinked a yokel mob! You complain that he evaded your questions. Of course he did, and did it perfectly! Ask him about the labor problem, and he replies, "I believe in democracy." Ask his views on religion, and he says, "Love thy neighbor as thyself." Now —you know you couldn't argue with that, either of you. I tell you, gentlemen, he's a vote-getter if I ever saw one. His very name is right—Abraham Lincoln! Honest Old Abe! He'll play the game with us now, and he'll go right on playing it when we get him into the White House. He'll do just what we tell him. . . .

DR. BARRICK (*cautioning him*)

Careful, Mr. Crimmin. . . .

(ABE *returns.*)

ABE

If you gentlemen will step into the dining-room, Mrs. Lincoln would be pleased to serve you with a cup of tea.

BARRICK

Thank you.

STURVESON

This is most gracious.

(*He and* BARRICK *move off toward the door.*)

ABE

Or perhaps something stronger for those who prefer it.

(STURVESON *and* BARRICK *go.* CRIMMIN *is looking for a place to throw his cigar.*)

ABE (*heartily*)

Bring your seegar with you, Mr. Crimmin!

CRIMMIN

Thank you—thank you!
(*He smiles at* ABE, *gives him a slap on the arm, and goes out,* ABE *following. The lights fade.*)

END OF SCENE X

SCENE XI

Lincoln campaign headquarters in the Illinois State House. The evening of Election Day, November 6th, 1860.

It is a large room with a tall window opening out on to a wide balcony. There are doors upper right and upper left. At the left is a table littered with newspapers and clippings. There are many chairs about, and a liberal supply of spittoons.

At the back is a huge chart of the thirty-three states, with their electoral votes, and a space opposite each side for the posting of bulletins. A short ladder gives access to Alabama and Arkansas at the top of the list.

On the wall at the left is an American flag. At the right is a map of the United States, on which each state is marked with a red, white or blue flag.

ABE is sitting at the table, with his back to the audience, reading newspaper clippings. He wears his hat and has spectacles on. MRS. LINCOLN is sitting at the right of the table, her eyes darting nervously from ABE, to the chart, to the map. She wears her bonnet, tippet and muff.

ROBERT LINCOLN is standing near her, studying the map. NINIAN EDWARDS is sitting at the left of the table and JOSH SPEED is standing near the chart. They are both smoking cigars and watching the chart.

The door at the left is open, and through it the clatter of telegraph instruments can be heard. The window is partly open, and we can hear band music from the square below, and frequent cheers from the assembled mob, who are watching the election returns flashed from a magic lantern on the State House balcony.

Every now and then, a telegraph operator named JED *comes in from the left and tacks a new bulletin up on the chart. Another man named* PHIL *is out on the balcony taking bulletins from* JED.

ROBERT

What do those little flags mean, stuck into the map?

JOSH

Red means the state is sure for us. White means doubtful. Blue means hopeless.

*(*ABE *tosses the clipping he has been reading on the table and picks up another.)*

*(*JED *comes in and goes up to pin bulletins opposite Illinois, Maryland and New York.)*

NINIAN *(rising to look)*

Lincoln and Douglas neck and neck in Illinois.

*(*JOSH *and* ROBERT *crowd around the chart.)*

JOSH

Maryland is going all for Breckenridge and Bell. Abe—you're nowhere in Maryland.

MARY (*with intense anxiety*)

What of New York?

JED (*crossing to the window*)

Say, Phil—when you're not getting bulletins, keep that window closed. We can't hear ourselves think.

PHIL

All right. Only have to open 'er up again. (*He closes the window.*)

MARY

What does it say about New York?
(JED *goes.*)

NINIAN

Douglas a hundred and seventeen thousand—Lincoln a hundred and six thousand.

MARY (*desperately, to* ABE)

He's winning from you in New York, Abe!

JOSH

Not yet, Mary. These returns so far are mostly from the city where Douglas is bound to run the strongest.

ABE (*interested in a clipping*)

I see the New York *Herald* says I've got the soul of a Uriah Heep encased in the body of a baboon. (*He puts the clipping aside and starts to read another.*)

Ninian (*who has resumed his seat*)

You'd better change that flag on Rhode Island from red to white, Bob. It looks doubtful to me.

(Robert, *glad of something to do, changes the flag as directed.*)

MARY

What does it look like in Pennsylvania, Ninian?

NINIAN

There's nothing to worry about there, Mary. It's safe for Abe. In fact, you needn't worry at all.

MARY (*very tense*)

Yes. You've been saying that over and over again all evening. There's no need to worry. But how can we help worrying when every new bulletin shows Douglas ahead.

JOSH

But every one of them shows Abe gaining.

NINIAN (*mollifying*)

Just give them time to count all the votes in New York and then you'll be on your way to the White House.

MARY

Oh, why don't they hurry with it? Why don't those returns come in?

ABE (*preoccupied*)

They'll come in—soon enough.

(BILLY HERNDON *comes in from the right. He*

has been doing a lot of drinking but has hold of himself.)

BILLY

That mob down there is sickening! They cheer every bulletin that's flashed on the wall, whether the news is good or bad. And they cheer every picture of every candidate, including George Washington, with the same, fine, ignorant enthusiasm.

JOSH

That's logical. They can't tell 'em apart.

BILLY (*to* ABE)

There are a whole lot of reporters down there. They want to know what will be your first official action after you're elected.

NINIAN

What do you want us to tell 'em, Abe?

ABE (*still reading*)

Tell 'em I'm thinking of growing a beard.

JOSH

A beard? NINIAN (*amused*)

Whatever put that idea into your mind?

ABE (*picking up another clipping*)

I had a letter the other day from some little girl. She said I ought to have whiskers, to give me more dignity. And I'll need it—if elected.

(JED *arrives with new bulletins.* BILLY, NINIAN,

JOSH *and* ROBERT *huddle around* JED, *watching him post the bulletins.*)

MARY

What do they say now?

(JED *goes to the window and gives some bulletins to* PHIL.)

MARY

Is there anything new from New York?

NINIAN

Connecticut—Abe far in the lead. That's eleven safe electoral votes anyway. Missouri—Douglas thirty-five thousand—Bell thirty-three—Breckenridge sixteen—Lincoln, eight. . . .

(*Cheers from the crowd outside until* PHIL *closes the window.* JED *returns to the office at the left.*)

MARY

What are they cheering for?

BILLY

They don't know!

ABE (*with another clipping*)

The Chicago *Times* says, "Lincoln breaks down! Lincoln's heart fails him! His tongue fails him! His legs fail him! He fails all over! The people refuse to support him! They laugh at him! Douglas is champion of the people! Douglas skins the living dog!"

(*He tosses the clipping aside.* MARY *stands up.*)

MARY (*her voice is trembling*)

I can't stand it any longer!

ABE

Yes, my dear—I think you'd better go home. I'll be back before long.

MARY (*hysterical*)

I won't go home! You only want to be rid of me. That's what you've wanted ever since the day we were married—and before that. Anything to get me out of your sight, because you hate me! (*Turning to* JOSH, NINIAN *and* BILLY.) And it's the same with all of you—all of his friends—you hate me— you wish I'd never come into his life.

JOSH

No, Mary.

(ABE *has stood up, quickly, at the first storm signal. He himself is in a fearful state of nervous tension—in no mood to treat* MARY *with patient indulgence. He looks sharply at* NINIAN *and at the others.*)

ABE

Will you please step out for a moment?

NINIAN

Certainly, Abe.

(*He and the others go into the telegraph office.* JOSH *gestures to* ROBERT *to go with them.* ROBERT *casts a black look at his mother and goes. . . .* ABE *turns on* MARY *with strange savagery.*)

ABE

Damn you! Damn you for taking every opportunity you can to make a public fool of me—and
yourself! It's bad enough, God knows, when you
act like that in the privacy of our own home. But
here—in front of people! You're not to do that
again. Do you hear me? You're never to do that
again!

(MARY *is so aghast at this outburst that her
hysterical temper vanishes, giving way to blank
terror.*)

MARY (*in a faint, strained voice*)

Abe! You cursed at me. Do you realize what
you did? You cursed at me.

(ABE *has the impulse to curse at her again, but
with considerable effort, he controls it.*)

ABE (*in a strained voice*)

I lost my temper, Mary. And I'm sorry for it.
But I still think you should go home rather than
endure the strain of this—this Death Watch.

(*She stares at him, uncomprehendingly, then
turns and goes to the door.*)

MARY (*at the door*)

This is the night I dreamed about, when I was a
child, when I was an excited young girl, and all the
gay young gentlemen of Springfield were courting
me, and I fell in love with the least likely of them.
This is the night when I'm waiting to hear that my

husband has become President of the United States. And even if he does—it's ruined, for me. It's too late. . . .

(*She opens the door and goes out.* ABE *looks after her, anguished, then turns quickly, crosses to the door at the left and opens it.*)

ABE (calling off)

Bob!

(ROBERT *comes in.*)

Go with your Mother.

ROBERT

Do I have to?

ABE

Yes! Hurry! Keep right with her till I get home.

(ROBERT *has gone.* ABE *turns to the window.* PHIL *opens it.*)

PHIL

Do you think you're going to make it, Mr. Lincoln?

ABE

Oh—there's nothing to worry about.

CROWD OUTSIDE (singing)

Old Abe Lincoln came out of the wilderness
    Out of the wilderness
    Out of the wilderness
Old Abe Lincoln came out of the wilderness
    Down in Illinois!

(NINIAN, JOSH, BILLY, AND JED *come in, the lat-*
ter to post new bulletins. After JED *has communi-*
cated these, PHIL *again closes the window.* JED
goes.)

NINIAN

It looks like seventy-four electoral votes sure
for you. Twenty-seven more probable. New York's
will give you the election.

(ABE *walks around the room.* JOSH *has been*
looking at ABE.)

JOSH

Abe, could I get you a cup of coffee?

ABE

No, thanks, Josh.

NINIAN

Getting nervous, Abe?

ABE

No. I'm just thinking what a blow it would be
to Mrs. Lincoln if I should lose.

NINIAN

And what about me? I have ten thousand dollars bet on you.

BILLY (*scornfully*)

I'm afraid that the loss to the nation would be
somewhat more serious than that.

JOSH

How would you feel, Abe?

ABE (*sitting on the chair near the window*)

I guess I'd feel the greatest sense of relief of my life.

(JED *comes in with a news despatch.*)

JED

Here's a news despatch. (*He hands it over and goes.*)

NINIAN (*reads*)

"Shortly after nine o'clock this evening, Mr. August Belmont stated that Stephen A. Douglas has piled up a majority of fifty thousand votes in New York City and carried the state."

BILLY

Mr. Belmont be damned!

(CRIMMIN *comes in, smoking a cigar, looking contented.*)

CRIMMIN

Good evening, Mr. Lincoln. Good evening, gentlemen—and how are you all feeling *now?*

(*They all greet him.*)

NINIAN

Look at this, Crimmin. (*He hands the despatch to* CRIMMIN.)

CRIMMIN (*smiles*)

Well—Belmont is going to fight to the last ditch, which is just what he's lying in now. I've been in Chicago and the outlook there is cloudless. In fact, Mr. Lincoln, I came down tonight to protect you from the office-seekers. They're lining up down-stairs already. On the way in I counted four Ministers to Great Britain and eleven Secretaries of State.

(JED *has come in with more bulletins to put on the chart and then goes to the window to give* PHIL *the bulletins.*)

BILLY (*at the chart*)

There's a bulletin from New York! Douglas a hundred and eighty-three thousand—Lincoln a hundred and eighty-*one* thousand!

(JED *goes.*)

JOSH

Look out, Abe. You're catching up!

CRIMMIN

The next bulletin from New York will show you winning. Mark my words, Mr. Lincoln, this election is all wrapped up tightly in a neat bundle, ready for delivery on your doorstep tonight. We've fought the good fight, and we've won!

ABE (*pacing up and down the room*)

Yes—we've fought the good fight—in the dirtiest campaign in the history of corrupt politics. And if I have won, then I must cheerfully pay my political debts. All those who helped to nominate and elect me must be paid off. I have been gambled all around, bought and sold a hundred times. And now I must fill all the dishonest pledges made in my name.

NINIAN

We realize all that, Abe—but the fact remains that you're winning. Why, you're even beating the coalition in Rhode Island!

ABE

I've got to step out for a moment. (*He goes out at the right.*)

NINIAN (*cheerfully*)

Poor Abe.

CRIMMIN

You gentlemen have all been close friends of our Candidate for a long time so perhaps you could answer a question that's been puzzling me considerably. Can I possibly be correct in supposing that he doesn't want to win?

JOSH

The answer is—yes.

CRIMMIN (*looking toward the right*)

Well—I can only say that, for me, this is all a refreshingly new experience.

BILLY (*belligerently*)

Would *you* want to become President of the United States at this time? Haven't you been reading the newspapers lately?

CRIMMIN

Why, yes—I try to follow the events of the day.

BILLY (*in a rage*)

Don't you realize that they've raised ten thousand volunteers in South Carolina? They're arming them! The Governor has issued a proclamation saying that if Mr. Lincoln is elected, the State will secede tomorrow, and every other state south of the Dixon line will go with it. Can you see what that means? War! Civil War! And *he'll* have the whole terrible responsibility for it—a man who has never wanted anything in his life but to be let alone, in peace!

NINIAN

Calm down, Billy. Go get yourself another drink. (JED *rushes in.*)

JED

Mr. Edwards, here it is! (*He hands a news despatch to* NINIAN, *then rushes to the window to attract* PHIL's *attention and communicate the big news.*)

NINIAN (*reads*)

"At 10:30 tonight the New York *Herald* conceded that Mr. Lincoln has carried the state by a majority of at least twenty-five thousand and has won the election!" (*He tosses the despatch in the air.*) He's won! He's won! Hurrah!

(*All on the stage shout, cheer, embrace and slap each other.*)

BILLY

God be praised! God be praised!

CRIMMIN

I knew it! I never had a doubt of it!

(JED *is on the balcony, shouting through a megaphone.*)

JED

Lincoln is elected! Honest Old Abe is our next President!

(*A terrific cheer ascends from the crowd below.* ABE *returns. They rush at him.* BILLY *shakes hands with him, too deeply moved to speak.*)

NINIAN

You've carried New York, Abe! You've won! Congratulations!

CRIMMIN

My congratulations, Mr. President. This is a mighty achievement for all of us!

(JED *comes in and goes to* ABE.)

JED

My very best, Mr. Lincoln!

ABE (*solemnly*)

Thank you—thank you all very much.

(*He comes to the left.* JOSH *is the last to shake his hand.*)

JOSH

I congratulate you, Abe.

ABE

Thanks, Josh.

NINIAN

Listen to them, Abe. Listen to that crazy, howl-ing mob down there.

CRIMMIN

It's all for you, Mr. Lincoln.

NINIAN

Abe, get out there and let 'em see you!

ABE

No. I don't want to go out there. I—I guess I'll be going on home, to tell Mary. (*He starts toward the door.*)

(*A short, stocky officer named* KAVANAGH *comes in from the right. He is followed by two soldiers.*)

CRIMMIN

This is Captain Kavanagh, Mr. *President*.

KAVANAGH (*salutes*)

I've been detailed to accompany you, Mr. Lin-coln, in the event of your election.

ABE

I'm grateful, Captain. But I don't need you.

KAVANAGH

I'm afraid you've got to have us, Mr. Lincoln. I don't like to be alarming, but I guess you know as well as I do what threats have been made.

ABE (*wearily*)

I see . . . Well—Good night, Josh—Ninian—Mr.

Crimmin—Billy. Thank you for your good wishes.

(He starts for the door. The others bid him good night, quietly.)

KAVANAGH

One moment, Sir. With your permission, I'll go first.

(He goes out, ABE after him, the two other soldiers follow. The light fades.)

END OF SCENE XI

SCENE XII

*The yards of the railroad station at Springfield.
The date is February 11, 1861.*

*At the right, at an angle toward the audience, is
the back of a railroad car. From behind this, off
to the upper left, runs a ramp. Flags and
bunting are draped above.*

*In a row downstage are soldiers, with rifles and
bayonets fixed, and packs on their backs, standing
at ease. Off to the left is a large crowd, whose excited murmuring can be heard.*

*KAVANAGH is in the foreground. A BRAKEMAN
with a lantern is inspecting the wheels of the car,
at the left. A WORKMAN is at the right, polishing
the rails of the car. KAVANAGH is pacing up and
down, chewing a dead cigar. He looks at his watch.
A swaggering MAJOR of militia comes down the
ramp from the left.*

MAJOR

I want you men to form up against this ramp.
(*To* KAVANAGH; *with a trace of scorn.*) You seem
nervous, Mr. Kavanagh.

KAVANAGH

Well—I am nervous. For three months I've been
guarding the life of a man who doesn't give a damn

177

what happens to him. I heard today that they're betting two to one in Richmond that he won't be alive to take the oath of office on March the 4th.

MAJOR

I'd like to take some of that money. The State Militia is competent to protect the person of our Commander-in-Chief.

KAVANAGH

I hope the United States Army is competent to help. But those Southerners are mighty good shots. And I strongly suggest that your men be commanded to keep watch through every window of every car, especially whenever the train stops—at a town, or a tank, or anywhere. And if any alarm is sounded, at any point along the line . . .

MAJOR (*a trifle haughty*)

There's no need to command my men to show courage in an emergency.

KAVANAGH

No slur was intended, Major—but we must be prepared in advance for everything.

(*A brass band off to the left strikes up the campaign song, "Old Abe Lincoln came out of the wilderness." The crowd starts to sing it, more and more voices taking it up. A* CONDUCTOR *comes out of the car and looks at his watch. There is a commotion at the left as* NINIAN *and* ELIZABETH ED- WARDS, *and* JOSH, BILLY *and* CRIMMIN *come in and are stopped by the soldiers. The* MAJOR *goes forward, bristling with importance.*)

MAJOR

Stand back, there! Keep the crowd back there, you men!

NINIAN

I'm Mr. Lincoln's brother-in-law.

MAJOR

What's your name?

KAVANAGH

I know him, Major. That's Mr. and Mrs. Edwards, and Mr. Speed and Mr. Herndon with them. I know them all. You can let them through.

MAJOR

Very well. You can pass.

(*They come down to the right. The* MAJOR *goes off at the left.*)

CRIMMIN

How is the President feeling today? Happy?

NINIAN

Just as gloomy as ever.

BILLY (*emotionally*)

He came down to the office, and when I asked him what I should do about the sign, "Lincoln and Herndon," he said, "Let it hang there. Let our clients understand that this election makes no difference to the firm. If I live, I'll be back some time, and then we'll go right on practising just as if nothing had happened."

ELIZABETH

He's always saying that—"If I live" . . .

(*A tremendous cheer starts and swells offstage at the left. The* MAJOR *comes on, briskly.*)

MAJOR (*to* KAVANAGH)

The President has arrived! (*To his men*) Attention! (*The* MAJOR *strides down the platform and takes his position by the car, looking off to the left.*)

KAVANAGH (*to* NINIAN *and the others*)

Would you mind stepping back there? We want to keep this space clear for the President's party.

(*They move upstage, at the right. The cheering is now very loud.*)

MAJOR

Present—Arms!

(*The soldiers come to the Present. The* MAJOR *salutes. Preceded by soldiers who are looking sharply to the right and left,* ABE *comes in from the left, along the platform. He will be fifty-two years old tomorrow. He wears a beard. Over his shoulders is his plaid shawl. In his right hand, he carries his carpet-bag; his left hand is leading* TAD. *Behind him are* MARY, ROBERT *and* WILLIE, *and the* MAID. *All, except* MARY, *are also carrying bags.*)

*She carries a bunch of flowers. When they come to
the car, ABE hands his bag up to the CONDUCTOR,
then lifts TAD up. MARY, ROBERT, WILLIE and the
MAID get on board, while ABE steps over to talk to
NINIAN and the others. During this, there is considerable commotion at the left, as the crowd tries
to surge forward.)*

MAJOR (*rushing forward*)

Keep 'em back! Keep 'em back, men!

(*The* SOLDIERS *have broken their file on the
platform and are in line, facing the crowd.* KAVA-
NAGH *and his men are close to* ABE. *Each of them
has his hand on his revolver, and is keeping a sharp
lookout.*)

KAVANAGH

Better get on board, Mr. President.

(ABE *climbs up on to the car's back platform.
There is a great increase in the cheering when the
crowd sees him. They shout:* "Speech! Speech!
Give us a speech, Abe! Speech, Mr. President!
Hurray for Old Abe!" *Etc. . . . * ABE *turns to the
crowd, takes his hat off and waves it with a half-
hearted gesture. The cheering dies down.*)

NINIAN

They want you to say something, Abe.

(*For a moment,* ABE *stands still, looking off to
the left.*)

ABE

My dear friends—I have to say good-bye to you.

I am going now to Washington, with my new whiskers—of which I hope you approve.

(The crowd roars with laughter at that. More shouts of "Good Old Abe!" In its exuberant enthusiasm, the crowd again surges forward, at and around the SOLDIERS, *who shout, "Get back, there! Stand back, you!")*

ABE *(to the* MAJOR)

It's all right—let them come on. They're all old friends of mine.

(The MAJOR *allows his men to retreat so that they form a ring about the back of the car.* KAVANAGH *and his men are on the car's steps, watching. The crowd—an assortment of townspeople, including some Negroes—fills the stage.)*

ABE

No one, not in my situation, can appreciate my feelings of sadness at this parting. To this place, and the kindness of you people, I owe everything. I have lived here a quarter of a century, and passed from a young to an old man. Here my children have been born and one is buried. I now leave, not knowing when or whether ever I may return. I am called upon to assume the Presidency at a time when eleven of our sovereign states have announced their intention to secede from the Union, when threats of war increase in fierceness from day to day. It is a grave duty which I now face. In preparing for it, I have tried to enquire:

what great principle or ideal is it that has kept this Union so long together? And I believe that it was not the mere matter of separation of the colonies from the motherland, but that sentiment in the Declaration of Independence which gave liberty to the people of this country and hope to all the world. This sentiment was the fulfillment of an ancient dream, which men have held through all time, that they might one day shake off their chains and find freedom in the brotherhood of life. We gained democracy, and now there is the question whether it is fit to survive. Perhaps we have come to the dreadful day of awakening, and the dream is ended. If so, I am afraid it must be ended forever. I cannot believe that ever again will men have the opportunity we have had. Perhaps we should admit that, and concede that our ideals of liberty and equality are decadent and doomed. I have heard of an eastern monarch who once charged his wise men to invent him a sentence which would be true and appropriate in all times and situations. They presented him the words, "And this too shall pass away." That is a comforting thought in time of affliction—"And this too shall pass away." And yet— (*Suddenly he speaks with quiet but urgent authority.*) —let us believe that it is not true! Let us live to prove that we can cultivate the natural world that is about us, and the intellectual and moral world that is within us, so that we may secure an individual, social and political prosperity,

whose course shall be forward, and which, while
the earth endures, shall not pass away. . . . I com-
mend you to the care of the Almighty, as I hope that
in your prayers you will remember me. . . . Good-
bye, my friends and neighbors.

(*He leans over the railing of the car platform
to say good-bye to* NINIAN, ELIZABETH, JOSH,
BILLY *and* CRIMMIN, *shaking each by the hand. The
band off-stage strikes up "John Brown's Body."
The cheering swells. The* CONDUCTOR *looks at his
watch and speaks to the* MAJOR, *who gets on board
the train. The crowd on stage is shouting "Good-
bye, Abe," "Good-bye, Mr. Lincoln," "Good luck,
Abe," "We trust you, Mr. Lincoln."*)

(*As the band swings into the refrain, "Glory,
Glory Hallelujah," the crowd starts to sing, the
number of voices increasing with each word.*)

(KAVANAGH *tries to speak to* ABE *but can't be
heard. He touches* ABE's *arm, and* ABE *turns on
him, quickly.*)

KAVANAGH

Time to pull out, Mr. President. Better get inside the car.

(*These words cannot be heard by the audience
in the general uproar of singing.* NINIAN, ELIZA—
BETH, JOSH *and* BILLY *are up on the station platform. The* SOLDIERS *are starting to climb up on
to the train.* ABE *gives one last wistful wave of his
hat to the crowd, then turns and goes into the car,*

followed by KAVANAGH, *the* MAJOR *and the* SOL-
DIERS. *The band reaches the last line of the song.*)

ALL (*singing*)

His soul goes marching on.

(*The* BRAKEMAN, *downstage, is waving his lantern. The* CONDUCTOR *swings aboard. The crowd
is cheering, waving hats and handkerchiefs. The
shrill screech of the engine whistle sounds from the
right.*)

CURTAIN

THE SUBSTANCE OF
"ABE LINCOLN IN ILLINOIS"

THE SUBSTANCE OF
"ABE LINCOLN IN ILLINOIS"

The purpose of these supplementary notes is to state the principal sources from which the material of this play and the conception of its various characters are derived; to attempt to tell what is the historical basis for each of the twelve scenes, and wherein and why I have departed from the recorded facts; to indicate the events which occurred between scenes; and also to give me an excuse for adding some information which I was unable, for one reason or another, to incorporate in the play's structure.

Not that I hope, in these notes, to establish a convincing case for myself as a learned biographer. The playwright's chief stock in trade is feelings, not facts. When he writes of a subject out of history, or out of today's news, he cannot be a scholarly recorder or a good reporter; he is, at best, an interpreter, with a certain facility for translating all that he has heard in a manner sufficiently dramatic to attract a crowd. He has been granted, by a tradition that goes back to the Kings of Thebes, considerable poetic license to distort and embellish the truth; and he generally takes advantage of far more license than he has been granted. The Cleopatra who actually existed may have borne no resemblance to the Cleopatra of Shakespeare's creation nor to the entirely different one of Shaw's, but no one now cares about that, even in Egypt.

However, in the case of a play about the development of the extraordinary character of Abraham Lincoln, a strict regard for the plain truth is more than obligatory; it is obviously desirable. His life as he lived it was a work of art, forming a veritable allegory of the growth of the democratic spirit, with its humble origins, its inward struggles, its seemingly timid policy of "live and let live" and "mind your own business," its slow awakening to the dreadful problems of reality, its battles with and conquest of those problems, its death at the hands of a crazed assassin, and its perpetual renewal caused by the perpetual human need for it. Furthermore, just as Lincoln's life needs no adornments of symbolism to make it pertinent, his character needs no romanticizing, no sentimentalizing, no dramatizing.

Lincoln's great achievement, most of which was accomplished by the echoes of his words, long after his death, was the solidification of the American ideal. But this is not a play about his achievement: it is, rather, a play about the solidification of Lincoln himself—a long, uncertain process, effected by influences some of which came from within his own reasoning mind, some from his surrounding circumstances, some from sources which we cannot comprehend. As many as possible of these influences are indicated in this play; the rest are left to the imagination of the audience, because they are beyond mine.

Like many others, I obtained my first instruction in Lincoln's life from Ida M. Tarbell, and in the events of his period from Albert Bushnell Hart, but it was not until I had read Carl Sandburg's *The Prairie Years* that I began to feel the curious quality of the complex man who, in his statement of the eternal aspirations of the human race, achieved a supreme tirumph of simplicity. It was Sandburg who guided me back to the main sources of Lincoln lore, made me wish to know more of the forces, from without him and from within, which shaped this strange, gentle genius. *The Prairie Years* is an incomparable portrait of Lincoln and of the young, boisterous America in which he grew up. It is the work of a faithful historian who is also a major poet. Here is one sentence of Sandburg's: "So the woman, Nancy Hanks, died, thirty-six years old, a pioneer sacrifice, with memories of monotonous, endless everyday chores, of mystic Bible verses read over and over for their promises, and with memories of blue wistful hills and a summer when the crab-apple blossoms flamed white and she carried a boy-child into the world."

The Prairie Years is published by Harcourt, Brace and Co., who are now publishing the completion of Mr. Sandburg's great work, *The War Years.*

The best short biography of Lincoln, in its understanding of the inner man, is Nathaniel Wright Stephenson's. The two volumes by Albert J. Beveridge, which cover Lincoln's life up to the time of the Douglas debates, contain the most complete sifting of all the existing evidence. Beveridge gives the precise record of Lincoln's career, but refrains from speculation as to his character.

These books provided the main modern sources for this play. I have also had reference to the excellent biographies by W. E. Barton and Lord Charnwood; to studies of Mary Todd Lincoln by Carl Sandburg and W. A. Evans; to *Lincoln's Rise to Power,* by William Baringer; and (for all sorts of material) to the *Dictionary of American Biography,* especially the admirable article on Lincoln by James G. Randall. There are hundreds more books that I could mention, but I haven't read them; and there was John Drinkwater's beautiful play, which I saw several times and admired greatly.

The two original authors to whose works all students of this subject must ever return were Lincoln himself and the odd little enthusiast who was his law partner, William H. Herndon.

Lincoln's *Complete Works* were compiled by

John G. Nicolay and John Hay and published in 1894. Herndon's letters and papers have come out gradually through the years—first in the Herndon and Weik biography (1889), then in Weik's *The Real Lincoln* (1922) ; and a new collection, Emanuel Hertz's *The Hidden Lincoln*, was published in 1938, after this play was written. Mr. Hertz's book is of enormous interest, although it contains some admittedly fantastic statements made by Herndon in his dotage when, broken in health and impoverished, he was trying desperately to think up something new and sensational to reveal about his mighty friend.

To Herndon we owe a debt of inestimable gratitude. Had it not been for him, only the most fragmentary knowledge of Lincoln's true character would have survived the bullet of John Wilkes Booth. Many revealing statements would never have been made or recorded, many all-important letters would have been lost. Lincoln would be today only the frozen saint of the statuary, and we should have but a small conception of his real greatness. He was, as Herndon said, "a shut-mouth man" when it came to discussing his own hidden emotions. Herndon himself was as close to Lincoln as any man could be for more than twenty years ; but he confesses that during this long association he could do no more than guess at what was going on behind that resistant exterior. First as clerk and then as partner, from 1839 to 1861,

Herndon shared the same small office with Lincoln; he was in intimate association with him through all the period of his law practice, his marriage to the ill-starred Mary Todd, his one unsuccessful term in Congress, the painfully deliberate arousing of his ambition, his reluctant enlistment in the national struggle, his debates with Douglas, his nomination and election to the Presidency. Immediately after Lincoln's death, Herndon devoted himself with all his energy and all his limited means to one task, which was the collection of every available scrap of evidence from those who had known Lincoln in the years before the nation took him and made him its most faithful servant. To gain a conception of the overwhelming importance of Herndon's accomplishment, you may read through the ten-volume biography written by Lincoln's secretaries, Nicolay and Hay, and you will find that while all the events, particularly those following Fort Sumter, are carefully chronicled, there is hardly one revealing word of the nature of Lincoln's tragic soul, of his relations with his wife and other women, of the doubts that hindered him and the fears that obsessed him.

Here is a passage from Herndon, as published for the first time by Mr. Hertz:

"This man, this long, tall, bony, homely, wiry, sad, gloomy man floated into our country in 1831, in a frail canoe down the north fork of the Sangamon River, friendless, penniless, powerless, and alone, begging for work in this city, ragged, struggling for the common necessaries of life. This man, this peculiar man, left us here in 1861 the President of the United States, backed by friends and power, by fame and all individual and national forces, and it is well to inquire into the how."

That was the mission of Herndon's life—inquiring into "the how" of "this peculiar man."

Herndon says further: "Mr. Lincoln was a kind of fatalist in some aspects of his philosophy, and skeptical in his religion. He was a sad man, a terribly gloomy one—a man of sorrow, if not of agony. This, his state, may have arisen from a defective physical organization, or it may have arisen from some fatalistic idea, that he was to die a sudden and terrible death. Some unknown power seemed to buzz about his consciousness, his being, his mind, that whispered in his ear: 'look out for danger ahead!' . . . He has said to me more than once: 'Billy, I feel as if I shall meet with some terrible end.' He did not know what would strike him, nor when, nor where, nor how hard; he was a blind, intellectual Samson, struggling and fighting in the dark against the fates. I say on my own personal observation that he felt this for years. Often and often I have resolved to make or get him to reveal the causes of his misery, but I had not the courage nor the impertinence to do it. . . . May I say that I have, many times thoroughly sympathized with Mr. Lincoln in his intense sufferings; but I dared not obtrude into the sacred ground of his thoughts. . . ."

There was evidently only one man in all of Lincoln's life who was permitted to catch more than a glimpse of that sacred ground, and that one man was Joshua Speed. If Herndon was Lincoln's Fidus Achates, Speed was his Horatio. There is a remarkable statement of the relationship of Lincoln and Speed in *The Prairie Years:*

"Joshua Speed was a deep chested man of large sockets with broad measurement between the ears. A streak of lavender ran through him; he had spots soft as May violets. And he and Abraham Lincoln told each other their secrets about women. Lincoln too had tough physical shanks and large sockets, also a streak of lavender, and spots soft as May violets."

To Speed, Lincoln revealed aspects of his being that were never made visible to any other man, or any woman; and Speed would probably have taken these secrets with him to the grave had they not been pried out of him by Herndon.

Speed wrote to Herndon: "Mr. Lincoln was so unlike all the men I had ever known before or seen or known since that there is no one to whom I can compare him." Another of Speed's observations has exerted a profound influence on the conception of Lincoln that is given in this play: "He must believe he was right, and that he had truth and justice with him, or he was a weak man; but no man could be stronger if he thought he was right."

Over the statue in the Lincoln Memorial in Washington are the beautiful words, "In this Temple as in the hearts of the people for whom he saved the Union the memory of Abraham Lincoln is enshrined forever." And for those who stand in that temple, their spirit of reverence must be immeasurably increased by the knowledge that he was "a man of sorrow, if not of agony," "a peculiar man," and when not quite sure that he was right, "a weak man."

While I have made a steadfast effort to reflect the character of Lincoln as truthfully as I can, I have been less faithful in the portraits of the other historical characters who appear in this play, although I don't think I have done any grave injustice to the memory of any of them (except possibly Stephen A. Douglas, of whom more later). These other characters had to be used, for dramatic purposes, not as people important in themselves but as sources of light, each one being present only for the purpose of casting a beam to illumine some one of the innumerable facets of Lincoln's spirit.

I confess that I should like to have had a lot more time in this play for development of the character of Mary Todd Lincoln. She too was a very strange and pathetic person, but her rôle could be only that of a symbol of her husband's glorious, tragic destiny.

Her early letters reveal that, as a young girl, she had unusual intelligence, culture, perception and humor. She was tremendously ambitious—snobbish, to a certain degree—and was courted by many young men of wealth, breeding and excellent prospects, but she chose, against the opposition of her family, to marry a shabby, poverty-stricken, coarse and generally shiftless lawyer, who could have had little to recommend him to the attention of a young lady. It is to be presumed that she loved him dearly and had abiding faith in him when there seemed scant reason for it.

She lived with him through eighteen years (preceding his election) which must have imposed an intolerable strain on her patience. She bore him four sons, suffered poverty and indignity and neglect. During most of this time, he apparently progressed nowhere. If he had his own plans or hopes for the future, it is evident that he communicated no substantial part of them to his wife.

When the wildest dream of her life at length came true, and Mrs. Lincoln entered the White House, she was freely snubbed by Eastern society, she was publicly deplored, she was even accused of treason because of her family connections with the Southern cause. One of her sons had died in Springfield, another died in Washington. She was beginning to be unmistakably insane. All through the night after the firing of the shot in Ford's Theatre she sat weeping, "uttering heartbroken exclamations," and when they finally told her that the end of Abraham Lincoln had come, she moaned, *"Oh my God, and I have given my husband to die!"*

I have put those words in italics because I think they contain a poignant revelation of character. It was as though, even in that moment of fierce, maniacal grief, she wanted above all else to assure herself, and posterity, "It was *I* who made him President!"

Five years later, her son Tad died. Her extravagance, which had always run to the purchase of frills and furbelows at the expense of adequate food for her own family, now ran to fantastic extremes; for instance, she bought dozens of pairs of window curtains which she carried about with her from one hotel to another. Ten years after her husband's death attorneys for Robert Todd Lincoln, her sole surviving son, entered a court application which began, "The petition of Robert T. Lincoln would respectfully represent that his mother, Mary Lincoln, widow of Abraham Lincoln, deceased, a resident of Cook County, is insane, and that it would be for her benefit and for the safety of the community that she should be confined."

She was brought into court, and the application was granted. The County Clerk filed papers marked "Mary Lincoln, Lunatic." Before she was taken away, she tried to commit suicide. She was later released through the intervention of her brother-in-law, Ninian Edwards; and, in 1882, in his Springfield house, where she had met and married Abe Lincoln, she died. Buried with her was her wedding ring, inscribed "A.L. to Mary, Nov. 4, 1842. Love is Eternal."

In one of the Herndon letters in *The Hidden Lincoln* are these remarks:

"I say, Lincoln told her *he did not love her*. The world does not know her, Mrs. L's sufferings, her trials, and the causes of things. Sympathize with her. I shall never rob Mrs. Lincoln of her justice —justice due her. Poor woman! She will yet have her rewards."

Herndon wrote these sympathetic words in 1866, when Mrs. L. (who never liked him) had many sufferings and trials still before her. She has never received the rewards, at least upon this earth, to which he believed her entitled. Indeed, the voices of the scandal-mongers of Washington in her own day have only tended to increase in volume throughout the years. Of late, the domestic troubles of the Lincolns have received the attention of psychiatrists; these two unhappy people provide wonderful specimens for the Freudians to dissect. But, as Sandburg so perfectly expresses it, "Both gossip and science have little to guide them in effecting a true and searching explanation of the married life of a slow-going wilderness bear and a cultivated, tempestuous wildcat."

Just how far the bear would have gone without

the wildcat is something we shall never know and don't need to worry about. To the student of history there should be no such word as "If."

I now go on to discussion of the various scenes as they come:

SCENE I (1833)

In the summer of 1831, when Lincoln was twenty-two, he arrived in New Salem, Ill., a village of fifteen log cabins. An election was being held when he drifted into town. One of the election clerks was a fairly prosperous young Easterner, named John McNamar, who was engaged to be married to the local belle, Ann Rutledge, daughter of the proprietor of the tavern and the mill. The other clerk was Mentor Graham, the neighborhood school teacher. McNamar was ill, and a substitute had to be found, so Graham asked the uncouth stranger if he could read and write. Lincoln replied that he could and was promptly pressed into service to help record the votes—the start of his political career and of a friendship with Mentor Graham which meant much to him.

Lincoln boarded with Graham and that good man sat up nights, teaching him the rudiments of grammar and later of all manner of subjects, from Shakespeare to surveying. "I know of my own knowledge," wrote R. B. Rutledge (Ann's brother), "that Graham did more than all others to educate Lincoln."   . .

Graham himself said of Abe, "He was the most studious, diligent strait forward young man in the pursuit of literature and a knowledge I have taught," and he added that all loved this pupil because he was one of "the most *companionable* persons you will ever see in this world." He also said that he had once had to talk Abe out of committing suicide.

In this first scene is reference to Lincoln's trips by flat-boat to New Orleans, and I have been asked why I did not make mention of his visit to the New Orleans slave market, his rage at the spectacle, and his oft-quoted remark, "Someday I shall hit this thing and hit it hard!" I left that out because I don't believe any of it. If Lincoln was determined at this early stage of his career to free the slaves there is no reliable evidence that he ever said so. Perhaps he did visit the slave market, and perhaps that horrid sight did start certain thoughts forming in his mind—but, if so, it was a long, long time before he was ready to utter them and act on them.

The reading of Keats's "On Death," which concludes this scene, is one demonstration of the use of the playwright's license, previously referred to. There is no record of Lincoln's having read this poem. It is in keeping, however, with his taste in verse. He naturally had a great fondness for the sombre, his favorite poem being the one which started,

"Oh, why should the spirit of mortal be proud?
Like a swift-fleeting meteor, a fast-flying cloud,
A flash of the lightning, a break of the wave,
He passes from life to his rest in the grave."

Scene 2 (1834)

Several of the characters in this scene—Ben Mattling, Trum Cogdal, Seth Gale and the subordinate Clary's Grove boys—are imaginary. Mattling is introduced solely to show that Lincoln knew men who had fought in the Revolution, and Seth Gale because he will be of importance in a later scene.

Joshua Speed is introduced prematurely. He is an important character in the play, and therefore should become known to the audience this early. Actually, he and Lincoln did not meet until the latter moved to Springfield, some two or three years later. Speed was a merchant there, a man of good family and superior education, and he described the meeting in the following terms:

"He came into my store, set his saddle-bags on the counter, and enquired what the furniture for a single bedstead would cost. I took slate and pencil, made a calculation, and found the sum for furniture complete would amount to seventeen dollars

in all. Said he: 'It is probably cheap enough; but
I want to say that, cheap as it is, I have not the
money to pay. But if you will credit me until
Christmas, and my experiment here as a lawyer
is a success, I will pay you then. If I fail in that,
I will probably not pay you at all.' The tone of
his voice was so melancholy that I felt for him.
I looked up at him and I thought then, as I think
now, that I never saw so gloomy and melancholy a
face in my life. I said to him, 'So small a debt
seems to affect you so deeply, I think I can suggest
a plan by which you will be able to attain your end
without incurring any debt. I have a very large
room and a very large double bed in it, which you
are perfectly welcome to share with me if you
choose.' 'Where is your room?' he asked. 'Upstairs,' said I. . . . Without saying a word he took
his saddle-bags on his arm, went upstairs, came
down again, and with a face beaming with pleasure
and smiles, exclaimed, 'Well, Speed, I'm moved.' "

Which odd story is evidence of one of the most
remarkable elements in Lincoln's life: his astonishing gift for achieving immediate popularity. He
was always able, and without any great expendi-
ture of effort, to gain the devotion, trust and en-
thusiastic support of almost any one he might
meet. What has made him so peculiarly loved in
retrospect must have stood out all over him and
made him loved instantaneously. Of course, some
of the tributes to his early charm, honesty and

high promise were made after he had come to glory, and so may be discounted; but there are many contemporary testimonials and there are the strange facts of his life to establish the paradox that whereas he spent his years, even his crowded years in the White House, in a state of miserable loneliness, he never wanted for friends.

There is a letter extant (in the Barrett collection) written by a settler in New Salem and dated September 17, 1835, which gives us a good picture of young Abe Lincoln: "The Post Master is very careless about leaving his office open and unlocked during the day—half the time I go in and get my papers, etc., without any one being there, as was the case yesterday. The letter was only marked 25, and even if he had been there and known it was double, he would not (have) charged me any more —luckily he is a very clever fellow and a particular friend of mine."

This was the overwhelming sentiment of the community; they were all "particular" friends of Abe's. When Lincoln was twenty-three years old, and only seven months after he had first come out of the wilderness to New Salem, he ran for the State Assembly. His first speech began, "Fellow Citizens, I presume you all know who I am—I am humble Abraham Lincoln." (Even then he was shrewdly emphasizing his humility; thirty years later *The New York Herald* compared him to Uriah Heep.) He continued, "My politics are short and sweet, like the old woman's dance," and concluded, with another display of diffidence, "If elected I shall be thankful; if not it will be all the same to me."

The vote of the citizens of New Salem for the stranger in their midst was as follows:

For Abraham Lincoln 205
For his Opponent (whoever he was) . . . 3

Of course, this overwhelming majority may have been attributable in part to the presence at the polls of the Clary's Grove boys, ready to do violence to any one who dared to vote against their friend Abe. But, says Beveridge, his "local popularity was so great that their combative support was neither needed nor displayed."

Equally eloquent of his position in the hearts of his neighbors was his ability to run into debt and to be trusted for it. Although penniless, and with no prospects, he was in debt $1100 as a result of the collapse of the grocery store. He got in much deeper before he began to get out. Sandburg tells a story: "He was sued for ten dollars owing on his horse; a friend let him have the ten dollars; the horse was saved. He was sued again, and his horse, saddle, bridle, surveying instruments were taken away. James Short, a Sand Ridge farmer, heard about it; he liked Lincoln as a serious student, a pleasant joker, and a swift corn-husker; he had told people, when Lincoln worked for him,

'He husks two loads of corn to my one.' Short
went to the auction, bought in the horse and outfit for $125.00, and gave them back to Lincoln,
who said, 'Uncle Jimmy, I'll do as much for you
some time.' "

Short was paid back some years later from the
earnings of the law practice in Springfield. The
last of the New Salem debts were settled, after
seventeen years, with money saved during Lincoln's one term in Congress.

There were many James Shorts in Lincoln's life,
glad to come forth with substantial expressions of
their faith in him; none of them was ever disap-
pointed.

Bowling Green was Justice of the Peace and
leading citizen of New Salem. An immensely fat,
hearty and sympathetic man, he loved and appre-
ciated Abe and was the first, undoubtedly, to stimu-
late his interest in the law. This new interest had
an important effect on Lincoln's character. Said
R. B. Rutledge, "I think that he never avoided men
until he commenced the study of law." It was the
first evidence of his abstraction, his tendency to
misanthropy.

Ninian Edwards was one of the leaders of the
early Illinois aristocracy. His father was ap-
pointed by President Madison as first Governor
of the Territory and was later elected Governor
of the State. He had also been Ambassador to
Mexico. Thus, young Ninian enjoyed inherited

prominence as well as wealth; and yet, when he and the unknown Lincoln campaigned on the same ticket for the State Assembly in 1836, Lincoln ran ahead of Edwards and all other candidates in the voting. Of Ninian Edwards, a contemporary (U. F. Linder) wrote: "He was naturally and constitutionally an aristocrat, and hated democracy . . . as the devil is said to hate holy water."

In the scene between Abe and Ann Rutledge occurs the line, "I'm a plain, common sucker with a shirt-tail so short I can't sit on it." It may interest the reader to know that this is the first line of the play which contains any of Lincoln's own words. The shirt-tail expression was one that he liked to quote from his father. The word "sucker" meant at that time a native of Illinois—like "Hoosier" of Indiana; the Barnum definition came into the American language later.

There is little in the available records to indicate that Lincoln's decision to run for the Assembly was influenced by his love for Ann Rutledge—although I don't think I'm stretching my license too far by suggesting this. There have been fabulous estimates of the effect of Ann Rutledge on Lincoln's entire life, but actually we know little. This whole affair has been so clouded by the mauve mists of romantic legend that it is impossible to say for sure whether Abe ever proposed marriage to Ann and, if so, whether he was ever accepted. She had been engagd to McNamar, whose real name turned

out to be McNiel. His rôle bears some resemblances
to the traditional one of the city slicker. He left
New Salem, to go back East and collect his family,
and he stayed away for so long that she naturally
felt she must abandon hope of him and look elsewhere for consolation. Perhaps Abe provided it;
perhaps she was inconsolable.

A short time after Ann's death McNamar returned to New Salem to prove the honorableness
of his intentions and claim his bride. Years later,
he said, "I never heard any person say that Mr.
Lincoln addressed Miss Ann Rutledge in terms of
courtship, neither her own family nor my own ac-
quaintances otherwise. I heard simply from two
prominent Gentlemen of my acquaintance and Personal friends that Mr. Lincoln was Grieved very
much at her death."

From all the testimony of those who were in the
neighborhood at the time we may draw the following conclusions about Ann Rutledge and her importance: she was an attractive girl; she inspired
deep emotions in the heart and the imagination of
Abraham Lincoln; and she died.

That is all that really matters: she died.

SCENE 3 (1835)

The reading of *Pickwick*, with which this scene
opens, is a slight anachronism, as publication of
Dickens's first and greatest work did not start
until 1836. More accurate is the reference in a

speech of Speed's to Abe's absorption in "Hamlet." Lincoln read the tragedies of Shakespeare with consuming interest at this time, and memorized long passages. He also read Voltaire, and Tom Paine's *Age of Reason*, and Constantine de Volney's *Ruins*, a strange diet for a postmaster in a frontier village, though not so strange when you know what he was to be. When he was in the White House, he wrote to the actor James H. Hackett, "For one of my age I have seen very little of the drama. The first presentation of *Falstaff* I ever saw was yours here. . . . Perhaps the best compliment I can pay is to say, as I truly can, I am very anxious to see it again. Some of Shakespeare's plays I have never read; while others I have gone over perhaps as frequently as any unprofessional reader. Among the latter are 'Lear,' 'Richard III,' 'Henry VIII,' 'Hamlet' and especially 'Macbeth.' I think nothing equals 'Macbeth.' It is wonderful. Unlike you gentlemen of the profession, I think the soliloquy in 'Hamlet' commencing 'Oh, my offense is rank,' surpasses that commencing 'To be or not to be.' But pardon the small attempt at criticism. I should like to hear you pronounce the opening speech of Richard III."

That soliloquy which Lincoln admired ends with the violent words:

"O wretched state! O bosom black as death!
O Limed soul, that struggling to be free
Art more engaged! Help, angels! Make assay!

Bow, stubborn knees, and, heart with strings of
    steel,
Be soft as sinews of the new-born babe!
All may be well."

One can see him, sitting at the edge of the forest,
reading excitedly, feeling some weird kinship with
those turbulent, blood-stained, eternally self-ques-
tioning princes of old, struggling to understand
them.

You may find a fine passage describing the
effects of Ann Rutledge's death on Lincoln in
Nathaniel Wright Stephenson's sensitive biography. Here is a quotation from it:

"The sunny Lincoln, the delight of Clary's
Grove, had vanished. In his place was a desolated
soul—a brother to dragons, in the terrible imagery
of Job—a dweller in the dark places of affliction.
It was his mother reborn in him. It was all the
shadowiness of his mother's world; all that frantic
revelling in the mysteries of woe to which, hitherto,
her son had been an alien.

"To the simple minds of the villagers, with their
hard-headed, practical way of keeping all things,
especially love and grief, in the outer layer of consciousness, this revelation of an emotional terror
was past understanding. Some of them, true to
their type, pronounced him insane . . .

"In this crucial moment, when the real base of
his character had been suddenly revealed—all the

passionateness of the forest shadow, the unfathomable gloom laid so deep at the bottom of his soul—he was carried through his spiritual eclipse by the loving comprehension of two fine friends . . . two people who deserve to be remembered—Bowling Green and his wife . . .

"Ever after, at heart, he was to dwell alone, facing, silent, those inscrutable things which to the primitive mind are things of every day. Always, he was to have for his portion in his real self, the dimness of twilight, or at best, the night with its stars, 'never glad, confident morning again.' "

In this scene the only words that may have been said by Lincoln (and even their authenticity is doubtful) are, "I can't bear to think of her out there alone." His embittered remarks about the prayers of the Rutledges—"the Lord giveth and the Lord taketh away"—are not unjustifiable. I have mentioned his tastes in reading at this time, and he himself now wrote a tract on religion which, had it survived, might well have made his name anathema to all church-going people. It was mercifully burned by a friend named Samuel Hill, who was also a suitor for the hand of Ann Rutledge.

1835–1840

Some five years pass between Scenes 3 and 4. It was a time for Lincoln of considerable transformation, of a maturing process accelerated by contact with a new world. He changed from a backwoods-man into a townsman. Later he said that even be-fore he was thirty years of age he was considered "an old man."

He left New Salem forever and moved to Spring-field where he entered law practice as partner of Judge John T. Stuart. He indulged in a romance (if such it could be called) with a Miss Mary Owens. Neither of them took it very seriously. More important to his career were his first meet-ings and clashes with "The Little Giant," Stephen A. Douglas, who had moved to Illinois from his native Vermont and was now serving in the Assem-bly with Lincoln and voting against him—though not on the issue which was to bring these two men in historic opposition in the great debates of 1858 and the Presidential campaign of 1860.

Lincoln made a speech at this time in which he said, "The subject heretofore and now to be dis-cussed is the subtreasury scheme of the present administration, as a means of collecting, safe-keep-ing, transferring, and disbursing the revenues of the nation, as contrasted with a national bank for the same purposes. Mr. Douglas has said that we (the Whigs) have not dared to meet them (the Locos) in argument on this question. I protest against this assertion." Lincoln and Douglas be-came very heated on fiscal matters (these were the days of Andrew Jackson and his heir, Martin Van Buren) but there was not a word about slavery.

Beveridge says, "although advertisements of run-
away slaves were conspicuous in the Vandalia
newspapers and appeared with increasing fre-
quency, no one did or said anything about the
matter." But, in Boston, William Lloyd Garrison
had been shouting, "I am in earnest, I will not
equivocate, I will not excuse, I will not retreat a
single inch, and I WILL BE HEARD!" If Lincoln and Douglas did hear him, they probably
agreed, over a drink (Douglas's), that he was a
dangerous radical who should be suppressed. However, Lincoln collaborated with one Dan Stone on
a resolution which declared that "the institution of
slavery is founded on both injustice and bad policy,
but that the promulgation of abolition doctrines
tends rather to increase than abate its evils."

Lincoln's main activity at this time was in
political manœuvring to promote the transfer of
the State Capital from Vandalia to Springfield.
He helped to accomplish that, by a display of considerable skill as a lobby trader, and the citizens
of Springfield began to regard him as a favorite
son.

Scene 4 (1840)

The speech in which Lincoln describes seeing the
slaves on a river boat, chained together, is quoted
almost verbatim from a letter he wrote to Joshua
Speed's sister. The joke about the two d's in Todd
was his own and typical of his humor which, be it

said, was not always animated by a spirit of malice toward none. It has often been said of him, "His wit was always kindly; he never hurt any one with his quips." I believe Lincoln would resent that.

Reference is made to the Black Hawk War, in which Lincoln led a company of New Salem volunteers, including Jack Armstrong as sergeant. That was in 1832. The company saw no action, but they did meet the author of *Thanatopsis*, William Cullen Bryant, who was making a tour of Illinois for *The New York Evening Post*. He described Lincoln as "a raw youth" of "quaint and pleasant talk." During this brief campaign Abe encountered for the first time the difficulties of leadership. With his little company, he came up to a fence and realized that he didn't know the correct military command for getting over it. He pondered the problem for a moment, then said, "The company will now fall out, and will immediately fall in again on the other side of the fence." This was the sum total of his military experience before he became Commander-in-Chief of the army and navy of the United States in the first great war fought under modern conditions.

In the fourth scene, Lincoln's speeches expressive of his reluctance to become involved in national affairs indicate a breadth of interest which he can hardly be said to have displayed at this time (1840). However, this happened to be the only place within the play's structure where he could reasonably express the point of view which was to be his when, a few years later, he served in Congress and gained great unpopularity by opposing the Mexican War. There again he was opposed by Douglas who shouted for the war, quoting Frederick the Great, "Take possession first and negotiate afterward." Lincoln denounced the whole project as a land grab, which it was.

Scene 5 (1840)

One of the many people from whom Herndon obtained statements was Elizabeth Todd Edwards, wife of Ninian. Here is her description of the strange courtship of her sister by Abraham Lincoln:

"I have often happened in the room where they were sitting and Mary invariably led the conversation. Mr. Lincoln would sit at her side and listen. He scarcely said a word but gazed on her as if irresistibly drawn to her by some superior and unseen power. He could not maintain himself in a continued conversation with a lady reared as Mary was. He was not educated and equipped mentally to make himself either interesting or attractive to the ladies. He was a good, honest, and sincere young man whose rugged manly qualities I admired; but to me he somehow seemed ill-constituted by nature and education to please such a woman as my sister. Mary was quick, gay, and in the social world somewhat brilliant. She loved show and power, and was the most ambitious woman I ever knew. She used to contend when a girl, to her friends in Kentucky, that she was destined to marry a President. I have heard her say that myself, and after mingling in society in Springfield she repeated the semingly absurd and idle boast. Although Mr. Lincoln seemed to be attached to Mary, and fascinated by her wit and sagacity, yet I soon began to doubt whether they could always be so congenial. In a short time I told Mary my impression that they were not suited, or, as some persons who believe matches are made in heaven would say, not intended for each other."

Subsequent events proved Mrs. Edwards eminently correct in assuming that they were "not suited." But those who believe in the will of God, or those metaphysicians who believe in the existence of inexorable psychic forces, will maintain they most certainly were "intended."

Scene 6 (1841)

The episode of the burned letter in this scene is not an invention, as some who have seen this play have supposed. For some time before the date set for the wedding, Lincoln had been casting about desperately for a means of escape, and Mary Todd had attempted to transform him from the pursued to the pursuer by means of the ancient device of stimulating jealousy: she flirted conspicuously with other men, especially Douglas. This failed to have the desired effect on Lincoln; perhaps he didn't even notice what she was up to. He did what many other men have done in their cowardly but understandable desire to avoid a distasteful scene —he put his sentiments down on paper and gave that paper to a friend for delivery.

Of this letter, Joshua Speed has said: "In it he made a plain statement of his feelings, telling her that he had thought the matter over calmly and with deep deliberation, and now felt that he did not love her sufficiently to warrant her in marrying him. This letter he desired me to deliver. Upon my declining to do so he threatened to intrust it to some other person's hand. . . . Thereupon I threw the unfortunate letter in the fire. 'Now,' I continued, 'if you have the courage of manhood, go to see Mary yourself; tell her, if you do not love her, the facts.' . . . Thus admonished, he buttoned his coat, and with a rather determined look started out to perform the serious duty."

There is plenty of testimony to the resultant state of Lincoln's mind. "Restless, gloomy, miserable, desperate, he seemed an object of pity," wrote Herndon. "Knives and razors, and every instrument that could be used for self-destruction were removed from his reach," said Speed. "Lincoln went as crazy as a loon," said Ninian Edwards. And Lincoln himself wrote to his law partner, Judge Stuart: "I have within the last few days, been making a most discreditable exhibition of myself in the way of hypochondriacism . . . I am now the most miserable man living. If what I feel were distributed to the whole human family, there would not be one cheerful face left on earth. Whether I shall ever be better, I cannot tell; I awfully forbode I shall not. To remain as I am is impossible; I must die or be better, it appears to me."

Reference is made in this scene to Doctor Daniel Drake, to whom Lincoln was recommended at that time. Lincoln did not go to Cincinnati to see him, but sent him a long letter, detailing all his symptoms. Most of this letter was read to Speed before it was posted, but there was one portion so personal that Lincoln wouldn't reveal it even to his trusted friend. Speed romantically believed that this unknown part of the confession might have related to the tragic loss of Ann Rutledge, but Speed was merely guessing. Herndon had another explanation. It is tantalizing to think that this letter does not survive today. Doctor Drake received it, and replied that he could not render an opinion without a personal examination. Perhaps Lincoln asked him to destroy the letter and he did so. He was one of the great leaders of his profession, founder of the Ohio Medical College, and a keen historian of pioneer days in the Middle West; it is a great shame that he could not have known Lincoln's letter was the most important historical document that ever came before his eyes.

The outburst of Herndon toward the end of this sixth scene is an imaginary interlude. Herndon was a hot-headed radical, devoted to the memory of the martyred Lovejoy, and he has confessed that he wanted many times to talk thus to Lincoln; but there is no indication that he ever had the courage to do so, even aided (as he so frequently was) by strong drink. However, there is every reason in the world to believe that Lincoln said such things to himself, again and again, with increasing fervor as the years went on, until the time came when he could no longer refrain from saying them out loud.

SCENE 7 (1842)

Of all the twelve scenes, this one is the most completely fictitious, and the one which presented the greatest difficulty in the writing. It requires explanation.

It is obvious that, in the course of his life, Lincoln underwent an astonishing metamorphosis, from a man of doubt and indecision—even of indifference—to a man of passionate conviction and decisive action. This metamorphosis was not accomplished in one stroke, by one magnificent act of God. It was so slow and gradual that its progress was not visible to any one, even (in all likelihood) to Lincoln himself. What caused it?

Perhaps, in this play, I have exaggerated the fact that he was forever pushed forward by his wife and his friends. Certainly, they were always trying—they were expressing, however unconsciously, the need of the people of their shuddering country for a leader who was a man of the people—but for a long time he successfully resisted them. When he did go forward, it was entirely under his own steam. But what were the deep fires of wrath that produced that steam?

In this seventh scene, I had to try to suggest the answer to that question.

We know that Lincoln was always opposed to slavery in theory, but he was even more opposed to the stirring up of trouble—and he knew that in the slave question were stores of high explosive which, if ignited, could destroy the Union. He was not one to go examining those stores with lighted matches. He would never have lifted his finger, or raised his voice, to deprive the Southerners of their right to hold their own property. In so far as he was concerned, North and South could go on living together, harmoniously, half slave and half free. He vaguely hoped that, somehow or other, the slave problem would work itself out.

But—in these stirred, troubled years, the United States was refusing to remain as it had been, divided into North and South. The wheels of the covered wagons were beginning to cut long furrows across the plains beyond the Mississippi River. Lincoln could hear the rumble of those wagons. He crossed their trails many times, when he was out on the circuit, when he was travelling down to Kentucky to visit Josh Speed's family and recover from his "hypochondriacism." Settlers were pouring through Missouri and Iowa into Kansas and Nebraska; they were even starting to travel overland to the remote Pacific Coast. The Republic of Texas was hammering for admission to the Union.

Lincoln had frequent contact with the drivers of those covered wagons. In the very depths of his nature, in the very chemistry of his blood, he was one of them, a carrier of the progressive spirit that makes men restless and turns them into pioneers. So it was a personal matter to him when he heard increasingly hot arguments as to whether all this vast new territory of the West should be slave or free. This problem had been disposed of, temporarily, by the Missouri Compromise which, in effect, extended the Mason-Dixon Line on into the West; but Stephen A. Douglas helped to shatter that Compromise, and the Supreme Court handed down the Dred Scott decision. It was then that Lincoln began to move.

Said Herndon: "The repeal of the Missouri Compromise acts roused Lincoln—waked him up to his new opportunities and he seized them.

Thus, it was not the mere fact of slavery which converted Lincoln into the leader of a militant cause: it was the question of its extension. If he was willing to let the South mind its own business, he was not willing to stand by in silence when it threatened to establish domination of the West. He knew that the West would not accept such domination, and would fight back. The West was being settled by rebellious men, like Osawatomie John Brown.

I have tried, all through this play, from the first scene on, to provide evidence of Lincoln's awareness of the West, of his feeling of kinship for those who were to be its first settlers, and the sense of responsibility which he ultimately had to them. To crystallize all this, to indicate that Lincoln had at length made up his own mind and the influences that forced him to do it, is the purpose of this symbolic seventh scene. The prayer which Lincoln gives for a sick boy is, in effect, a prayer for the survival of the United States of America.

Scene 8 (1842)

All that can be said about this brief scene is that it seemed necessary. The chronology of the play, which had been fairly orderly and correct throughout the first six scenes, was completely disrupted in the seventh, so that Lincoln's return to Mary Todd is merely expressive of his acceptance of his destiny. The suggestion that he had made up his mind before his marriage is, of course, ridiculous. It actually took him twelve more years of searching thought and observation, as will be shown.

(1843–1858)

Four sons were born to the Lincolns—Robert Todd, in 1843; Edward, 1846, William Wallace, 1850; and Thomas ("Tad") 1852. Edward died when he was four.

(It is known that Lincoln wanted to name his first son after Joshua Speed, but this wish was over-ruled by the majority in the home and the boy was named after his maternal grandfather who had been a captain in the War of 1812 and a bank president in Kentucky. Robert justified his name, by following in the dainty footsteps of the Todds rather than the huge ones of the Lincolns. He was educated at Exeter and Harvard, served as Secretary of War under President Garfield, as Minister to London under President Harrison, became a successful corporation lawyer and president of the Pullman Company—in which capacity his hostility to the interests of labor indicated that he had not paid strict attention to the opinions of his father. He spent the last fifteen years of his life in retirement at his New Hampshire home, playing golf and saying "No" to all who begged him for access to the private papers which had come to him with his father's meager estate. Indeed, he decided to burn these papers and was restrained from doing so only by the timely intervention of Nicholas Murray Butler, who persuaded him at least to place them under seal in the Library of

Congress. Robert Lincoln left orders that they shall not be opened until 1976, when a new series of biographies and plays about Abraham Lincoln may be written.)

Two years after his marriage, Lincoln revisited scenes of his youth in Indiana and was moved to write some mournful doggerel, in the mood of Gray's *Elegy*. Here are two of the twenty-four stanzas:

> "I hear the lone survivors tell
>   How naught from death could save,
> Till every sound appears a knell
>   And every spot a grave—
>
> "I range the fields with pensive tread
>   I pace the hollow rooms;
> And feel (companion of the dead)
>   I'm living in the tombs—"

In 1846 he ran for Congress, without much enthusiasm, and was elected. A letter to Joshua Speed at this time indicated how marriage had parted these two friends: "You, no doubt, assign the suspension of our friendship to the true philosophic cause; though it must be confessed by both of us that this is rather a cold reason for allowing a friendship such as ours to die by degrees . . . Being elected to Congress, though I am very grateful to our friends for having done it, has not pleased me as much as I expected."

As has been said, Lincoln's one term in Congress was not a success. He breakfasted in the home of Daniel Webster, whose reply to Hayne had thrilled him when he was barely twenty-one, and he attracted the attention of Horace Greeley who was then, in *The New York Tribune*, pointing with indignation at Congressmen who took too much for mileage from the taxpayers' pockets; Greeley said that Lincoln had taken $676.80 in excess of the proper mileage from Springfield to Washington.

On January 12, 1848, Lincoln gave a vibrant speech, attacking President Polk and the whole purpose of the Mexican War. This speech makes good reading today, embodying as it does the true spirit of his liberalism. It did not go well with his patriotic constituents. *The Illinois State Register* branded him as "a second Benedict Arnold," and he was not renominated. His political career seemed finished. But a singularly perceptive (though unfortunately anonymous) Washington correspondent of *The Baltimore Patriot*, hearing the homely man from Illinois speaking in Congress, wrote back to his paper, "Evidently there is music in that very tall Mr. Lincoln." Whoever this correspondent may have been, I hope he lived to know the Gettysburg Address, and to be proud of the sensitivity of his own ear.

A comment on Lincoln at this time was provided by Douglas: "Mr. Lincoln served with me in the

Legislature in 1836, when we both retired, and he subsided, or became submerged, and he was lost sight of as a public man for some years. In 1846, when Wilmot introduced his celebrated proviso, and the abolition tornado swept over the country, Lincoln again turned up as a member of Congress from the Sangamon district. I was then in the Senate, and was glad to welcome my old friend and companion. Whilst in Congress he distinguished himself by his opposition to the Mexican War, taking the side of the common enemy against his own country; and when he returned home he found that the indignation of the people followed him everywhere, and he was again submerged or obliged to retire into private life, forgotten by his former friends." It must have been particularly galling to Douglas, whose whole career was one of unremitting and conspicuous activity, that his old friend and companion could not seem to remain submerged.

Lincoln joined in resolutions of sympathy with the cause of Hungarian freedom—"*Resolved*, That in the opinion of this meeting, the immediate acknowledgment of the independence of Hungary by our government is due from American freemen to their struggling brethren, to the general cause of republican liberty." (He was always deeply concerned with the struggle for freedom, wherever it might be.) A few years later he wrote a "Fragment on Government" and said: "Government is a combination of the people of a country to effect certain objects by joint effort. The best framed and best administered governments are necessarily expensive" . . . and a "Fragment on Slavery": "Advancement—improvement in condition—is the order in a society of equals. As labor is the common burden of our race, so the effect of some to shift their share of the burden onto the shoulders of others is the great durable curse of the race."

A philosophy was slowly developing, a philosophy relentless in its thoroughness. Lincoln had the soul of a poet, but he had the mind of a pure scientist, and these may be said to have been his laboratory years. He would not acknowledge that he had seen things at all until he had seen them whole, and all the implications beyond them. That is why people who hear words of his repeated in this play are surprised at their "timeliness." Joshua Speed has recorded, "I once remarked to him that his mind was a wonder to me; that impressions were made on it and never effaced. 'No,' he said, 'you are mistaken; I am slow to learn and slow to forget what I have learned. My mind is like a piece of steel—very hard to scratch anything on it, and almost impossible after you get it there to rub it out.' "

In 1854, Lincoln decided that he was ready to go. His speech at Peoria in that year was the first that gained him any degree of national prominence. Indeed, it established him as a member of "the liberal party throughout the world" (the words are his own). He said that it was our duty to that liberal party to save our Union; and "succeeding millions of free happy people, the world over, shall rise up and call us blessed." The Peoria address is one of the great, heroic documents of human history, for it proclaimed that Abraham Lincoln, of Sangamon County, Illinois, was no longer a weak, hesitant man who was not quite sure that he had truth and justice on his side.

SCENE 9 (1858)

Douglas was running for re-election to the Senate and Lincoln was opposing him. Lincoln's opening gun in the campaign was his "House Divided" speech, which was considered so inflammatory, even by Lincoln's own supporters who read it in advance, that he was urged to tone it down; but the marks had been graven deep on that "piece of steel" and nothing could rub them out. Douglas answered this speech, many times, proclaiming in tones of thunder that Lincoln was preaching Civil War!

The people of Illinois were excited by this campaign—it was a good, hot one—and people in the East and the South were beginning to take note of it. In *The New York Tribune* Horace Greeley wrote, "We trust Messrs. Lincoln and Douglas will speak together at some of the most important widely accessible points throughout the State."

Lincoln decided shrewdly to act upon this suggestion and sent a note to Douglas, "Will it be agreeable to make an arrangement for you and myself to divide time, and address the same audiences the present canvass?" Douglas didn't think much of the idea. "Between you and me," he told friends, "I do not feel that I want to go into this debate. The whole country knows me and has me measured. Lincoln is comparatively unknown . . . Should I win, I shall gain but little. I do not want to go into a debate with Lincoln." Perhaps the country didn't know Lincoln—but Douglas did!

Despite Douglas's accountable reluctance, public opinion demanded the debates and they were held. There were seven of them, and each lasted three or more hours. The crowds were huge and vociferous. They cheered and laughed uproariously, and when either of the contestants scored a particularly telling point, they shouted "Hit him again!" They did hit each other, and not always above the belt. Reading these many long speeches in cold print today you realize that their authors were not the usual senatorial candidates; they were men of genuine intellectual stature. Theirs were profound statements of political and social philosophy, full of reason and knowledge of history. When one considers the temper of audiences of voters today, one wonders how these Illinois crowds had the patience to sit through such lengthy discussions of abstruse problems and even to maintain fervent enthusiasm to the end; but one must remember that the Illinoisans of 1858 did not enjoy the boons now conferred by the radio and moving pictures, and for them political meetings were rare sources of entertainment.

Douglas's speech in this ninth scene is compounded of several of his utterances, especially those on the subject of the Supreme Court; but he never did hurl at Lincoln the scornful remarks about the state of striking labor in the North. Charges such as those were frequently made then, and Lincoln answered them, but they came from the more extreme partizans of the Southern cause. I am regretfully aware that this scene does much less than justice to Douglas. Unlike his great opponent, he was not at his best in a speech lasting only a few minutes. He needed (and took) hours.

Lincoln's reply is also a patchwork of quotations and paraphrases from various speeches given by him during the debates and before them and after them, and some of it is from his letters. For instance, the lines about the right to revolution are from the First Inaugural, those about the right to strike from a speech delivered in Hartford, Conn., when that state was suffering from shoemakers' strikes and Douglas was blaming it on sectional warfare. The passage toward the end of this speech about the policy of indifference, which Lincoln said, "I can not but hate," is from the Peoria speech. The last words, of course, are from the opening of the "House Divided" speech.

On the subject of racial discrimination and oppression Lincoln spoke and wrote voluminously and explicitly. He was concerned not only with the immediate problem of Negro slavery, but with the consequences of its continued existence and of the authority for its extension given by the Supreme Court in the Dred Scott decision. As has been said in these notes, he realized all the implications, and when, speaking of these implications, he warned, with terrible earnestness, "I advise you to watch out," he knew what he was saying. There was, in his time, an organization which called itself the American Party, but which was generally known as the Know-nothing Party. It was dedicated to the proposition that only Protestants of pure Anglo-Saxon blood should rule America, that all Catholics, Jews and "foreigners" in general (including Germans) should be reduced to the status of Negroes. Lincoln wrote to Speed, "You inquire where I now stand. That is a disputed point . . . I am not a Know-nothing; that is certain. How could I be? How can any one who abhors the oppression of Negroes be in favor of degrading classes of white people? Our progress in degeneracy seems pretty rapid." Some of the words that followed in that same letter are quoted in this debate speech.

As to the Supreme Court, Lincoln assailed it angrily time and again for the Dred Scott decision. He accused it of prejudice, of error, of "following the election returns" (as did Mr. Dooley), even of falsehood and conspiracy. His remarks on that subject in this speech are mild compared to some of his more extended diatribes. I have included his quotation from Jefferson, which he used at least twice. He also quoted Jefferson as saying, of judges, "They have, with others, the same passion for party, for power, and the privilege of their corps."

Such sentiments as Lincoln expressed on the sacred subject of the Supreme Court would constitute political suicide for any candidate for national office today, but in this 1858 campaign he won the majority of the popular vote. However, the senatorial election had to be decided in the State Legislature and it was in Douglas's favor. This was no set-back for Lincoln. Every one knew that he had beat his lusty opponent all hollow. He was not yet taken seriously as a Presidential possibility, but his lengthy shadow was beginning to be noticed far beyond the boundaries of Sangamon County.

To those unfamiliar with the life of Douglas, a few words about him may be interesting: he was honorable, able, and a fine patriot, and it is rather sad to reflect that he is known today only as a doormat for a greater man. As we have seen, his path and Lincoln's crossed and re-crossed throughout a period of twenty-five years. They had even

courted the same girl. In 1860 their persistent
rivalry was to reach its fantastic culmination,
when they ran against each other for the Presidency. Douglas was beaten again, and finally, because his party was split three ways as a result of
his own decent refusal to compromise with the more
implacable proponents of slavery. After Lincoln's
election, Douglas came to him and offered his
services. They were accepted, and Douglas, together with Seward (another rival), helped Lincoln compose the First Inaugural Address. (There
was ghost-writing in high places even then.) When
that speech was delivered, at the Capitol in Washington, Douglas stood beside his old friend and
adversary and held his plug hat. After the start
of the Civil War, Douglas was again at Lincoln's
side, giving support and counsel. Knowing that
enthusiasm for the war and for the President was
insufficient among many people in the Northwest,
he volunteered to make a speaking tour through
that territory and whip them up.

In the article on Douglas by Allen Johnson in
the *Dictionary of American Biography* you may
read a description of the Little Giant's last stand:

"On April 25, he made a remarkable speech to
his own people in the Capitol at Springfield. Fifty
years later, men who had been his political op-
ponents could not speak of it without emotion . . .
His great sonorous voice reverberated through the
chamber until it seemed to shake the building,

stirring men and women to a frenzy of excitement. In a few weeks that great voice was still. Stricken soon after with typhoid fever, he battled resolutely as ever with this last foe, but succumbed on June 3, 1861, his last words a message to his two boys bidding them to obey the laws and support the Constitution."

Americans should honor his memory.

SCENE 10 (1860)

The three characters who enter this scene— Sturveson, Barrick and Crimmin—are of course apocryphal and not based on any of Lincoln's contemporaries. Their purpose in the play, obviously, is to represent the world into which the crossroads politician was being drawn.

Lincoln's views on religion, as expressed in his reply to Doctor Barrick, are taken from F. B. Carpenter's *Six Months at the White House with Abraham Lincoln*. Mrs. Lincoln once said of her husband, "He never joined a church, but he was still a religious man. But it was a kind of poetry in his nature, and he never was a technical Christian." That was as good a way as any of accounting for the manifold, unfathomable mysteries in Abraham Lincoln: "It was a kind of poetry in his nature." That is why Sandburg is the perfect biographer.

Later on, in Washington, Lincoln attended regularly the Presbyterian Church, but never joined it.

Stephenson has written, "His religion flowered in his later temper. It did not, to be sure, overcome his melancholy. That was too deeply laid. Furthermore, we fail to discover in the surviving evidences any certainty that it was a glad phase of religion. Neither the ecstatic joy of the wild women, which his mother had, nor the placid joy of the ritualist, which he did not understand, nor those other variants of the joy of faith, were included in his portion. It was a lofty but grave religion. . . ." In fact, a form of religion inherited from his forebears of Puritan New England but qualified by his own eternal doubts and broadened by his own essential liberalism. If he knew any form of spiritual gladness, it was what has been called by another descendant of the Puritans, Mr. Justice Oliver Wendell Holmes, "the secret isolated joy of the thinker."

Lincoln's most vigorous statements on the relationship of capital and labor were made in an address delivered to a gathering of Wisconsin farmers at the State Fair in Milwaukee on September 30th, 1859, and he repeated these statements and enlarged upon them in his Message to Congress in December, 1861. Near the beginning of the Milwaukee speech you may find a paragraph which is a superb example of his humor and his artful method of winning the attention and affection of a crowd of strangers. He said, "I presume I am not expected to employ the time assigned me in the mere flattery of the farmers as a class. My opinion of them is that, in proportion to numbers, they are neither better nor worse than other people. In the nature of things they are more numerous than any other class; and I believe there really are more attempts at flattering them than any other, the reason of which I can not perceive, unless it be that they can cast more votes than any other. On reflection, I am not quite sure that there is not cause of suspicion against you in selecting me, in some sort a politician and in no sort a farmer, to address you." (A year later, in the Presidential election, he carried Wisconsin by a handsome majority.)

This tenth scene (and I have mentioned this point before in these notes) may seem to over-emphasize Lincoln's shrinking from great responsibility, suggesting again that he never sought public office for himself, but was always being thrust into it by others. Such was not my intention in writing the play, but it is evidently the impression that has been conveyed to many.

It is true that Lincoln's friends always displayed more confidence in him than he did in himself, and that his *persona* (to employ just one word out of psychoanalysis) was that of a man who is reluctant to advance, indifferent to fame and fortune. Nevertheless, it is a mistake to assume that he never pulled any strings on his own behalf. He pulled many, and he did it with consummate skill.

He was, in fact, one of the most artful campaigners that ever lived. When he could finally make up his mind that he wanted office and that he was fitted for it he went about the getting of it in a manner that was infinitely crafty. I don't know just when the Presidential bee entered his bonnet, but it was probably a lot earlier than any one knew at the time. He wrote a great number of letters to influential men, choosing his words carefully so as not to commit himself but still managing to suggest that he might be available. All of these letters ended with strict injunctions to secrecy—"burn this," etc.—but fortunately his orders were not always obeyed. In politics, as in everything else (except perhaps his humor) he was a profoundly subtle man. But—in politics, as in everything else, he was a bewilderingly contradictory one.

He worked hard, if silently, to win the Republican nomination. He sent $100 to a Kansas friend to help him get to the Chicago Convention, and he enclosed many instructions with the money. Others of his friends, such as Judge David Davis, Orville H. Browning, Judge Stephen T. Logan, Norman B. Judd and Leonard Swett, many of whom had known him since the New Salem days, were in Chicago working furiously, bargaining, trading, playing off such masters of the craft as Thurlow Weed and Horace Greeley against one another, preparing one of the most astounding coups in the history of political chicanery. While the Convention was in session, Lincoln was in Springfield, playing handball and (according to Herndon) steadying his nerves with an occasional glass of beer. But he was in close touch with his own shock troops at the front.

Nobody of any prominence in the highest councils of the party thought that Lincoln had the remotest chance of winning the nomination. Seward was far in the lead, and certainly deserved to win. But Lincoln's strategy had been brilliantly prepared, and his lieutenants were not too heavily burdened with the scruples that have wrecked many a political boom. The crisis came during the night before the first ballot was taken. Judge Davis and the others were sweating and struggling to win various delegations, notably Pennsylvania's, by munificent offers of jobs. It was at that crucial moment that Lincoln let them down.

Whether his conscience triumphed over his political ambition, or his nerve failed him, he suddenly shrank back and refused to go through with the disreputable business. Davis telegraphed him that they could make a deal to capture the Pennsylvania delegates if Lincoln would promise the office of Secretary of the Treasury to that dubious politician, Governor Simon Cameron. Lincoln replied, "I authorize no bargains and will be bound by none." Later, at literally the eleventh hour, he sent a messenger to Chicago with a heavily underlined message, "Make no contracts that will bind me."

This strange reneging by their candidate caused consternation among the frantic men in Lincoln headquarters. Jesse K. Dubois said, "Damn Lincoln!" Judge Davis, more practically, said, "Lincoln ain't here, and don't know what we have to meet, so we will go ahead, as if we hadn't heard from him, and he must ratify it!"

So the corrupt bargains were made, and Lincoln gained the nomination, and he did ratify it—although with a bitterness that found expression in these words (which are quoted in the next scene): "They have gambled me all around, bought and sold me a hundred times. I can not begin to fill the pledges made in my name."

Cameron became Secretary of War in a cabinet which ranks amongst the worst that have ever sat about a White House table.

Nevertheless, if Lincoln played ball with the boys before he became President, he stopped it afterward. He provided many stunning surprises for those (including the estimable Seward) who thought he would be malleable, tractable, and take orders. There is probably no other Chief Executive in our history who so thoroughly deserved the term Chief. Lincoln came to rule with an iron hand, taking but little advice and no orders from any one. In this way he gained the hatred and the attempted insubordination of those who had thought he would be easily bossed, but he gained the admiration and the invaluable friendship of Seward.

A memorandum which Lincoln read to his Cabinet in the last year of the Civil War is eloquent: "I must myself be the judge how long to retain in and when to remove any of you from his position. It would greatly pain me to discover any of you endeavoring to procure another's removal, or in any way to prejudice him before the public . . . My wish is that on this subject no remark be made nor question asked by any of you, here or elsewhere, now or hereafter."

Thus the humble Illinois sucker. Eight hours after his death, leaders of the Republican Party gathered and discussed plans "to get rid of the last vestige of Lincolnism." (You will find a fine description of this in Claude G. Bowers' powerful, shocking book, *The Tragic Era*.) At that meeting of political gangsters the horrors of the Reconstruction Period were gleefully plotted. One of those present was George Washington Julian, chairman of the Committee of Public Lands in the House of Representatives, and it is to his long unpublished diary that we are indebted for the knowledge that among his associates "The hostility for Lincoln's policy of conciliation and contempt for his weakness" were "undisguised" and that "his death is a Godsend to our cause."

The boys in the back room were grateful to John

Wilkes Booth for killing that one, solitary, strong man whose policy was based on the belief that "a just and lasting peace" might be achieved "with malice toward none; with charity for all."

Any one who doubts that Lincoln was absolute ruler of the United States of America during four years of emergency has only to contemplate the chaotic orgy of corruption which followed his death. Andrew Johnson turned out to be an honorable man, but neither he nor Seward nor any one else in the administration had the personal power of control which went to the grave with Lincoln.

However—I'm straying far from this play.

Scene 11 (1860)

The Presidential election which was held on November 6, 1860, was the most terrific in its excitement in our history. Not that there was any particular uncertainty as to the count of the votes, for Lincoln's election was virtually assured; but the country knew that these ballots could start fires of hatred which might never be put out. As was said at the time, Southern patriots were working to gain victory in this election, but they would not accept defeat!

As the nation went to the polls that day, Lincoln could read in the newspapers that Governor Gist of South Carolina had recommended the use of all available means for arming every man in the State between the ages of eighteen and forty-five, urging the need for such drastic action because, as he told the Legislature, "of the probability of the election to the Presidency of a sectional candidate by a party committed to the support of measures which if carried out will inevitably destroy our equality in the Union, and ultimately reduce the Southern States to mere provinces of a consolidated despotism."

These sentiments were wildly cheered throughout the South and other States were preparing to take similar measures. Small wonder that Lincoln was moved to say that "the task before me is greater than that which rested on Washington."

It is worth remembering that no man ever assumed the Presidency with so little of experience in public life to guide him. All other Presidents down to the present day had gained some substantial prominence as statesmen, soldiers, or, at least, as vote-getters, before receiving nomination to the highest office. Even those Vice-Presidents who acceded through death—Tyler, Johnson, Arthur, Theodore Roosevelt and Coolidge—had far more in their records to recommend them than did Lincoln, who had served only in the State Assembly when he was in his twenties and one inconspicuous term in Congress when he was in his thirties, and had never done anything to reveal any degree of executive ability. But he faced the greatest task of them all. He had reason for nervousness on November 6, 1860.

In this eleventh scene is one speech that has been much criticized and deplored by good people who revere Lincoln's memory and who cannot believe that he ever cursed at his wife. There is certainly overwhelming evidence of the fact that, in the years in the White House, he treated the obstreperous Mrs. Lincoln with unfailing courtesy and tender considerateness. This was his public behavior and, so far as any one can know, his private behavior, as well.

Nevertheless, I did not feel that this play concerning a part of the tragedy of Lincoln's life would be complete in its attempted honesty if I did not include the admission that, on occasion, his monumental patience snapped. That it did, before the move from Springfield, there can be no doubt. Usually he met her tirades with stony silence, or abrupt departure, or with laughter (the most infuriating response of all). But Herndon records that at least once, when she had run him out of the house and was chasing him down Eighth Street, and they approached some churchgoers, he turned on her, picked her up, spanked her, and thrust her back into the house, saying, "There, now, stay in the house and don't be a damned fool before the people."

Feeling that one such outburst from Lincoln to his wife was necessary, I placed it in this scene on Election Night, considering that this was the most appropriate moment, with the nerves of both so severely strained.

In this eleventh scene is reference to the letter from a little girl suggesting that Lincoln should grow a beard. Her name was Grace Bedell, of New York, and Lincoln's reply to her, written two weeks before the election, was as follows:

"My dear little Miss: Your very agreeable letter of the 15th is received. I regret the necessity of saying I have no daughter. I have three sons —one seventeen, one nine, and one seven years of age. They, with their mother, constitute my whole family. As to the whiskers, having never worn any, do you not think people would call it a piece of silly affectation if I were to begin it now? Your very sincere well-wisher, A. Lincoln."

In the election, Lincoln received about 40 per cent of the popular vote, Douglas about 30 per cent, with the rest divided between Breckenridge and Bell. In the Electoral College, Lincoln had 180 votes to 123 for the other three.

Scene 12 (1861)

There is no exaggeration in the suggestion that Lincoln's life was constantly threatened after his election, or that he himself was unresponsive to the attempts to guard him from assassination. He knew that there were many brave, desperate men determined to prevent him from taking the oath of office on March 4th, but he protested against bodyguards by saying, "What's the use of putting up a gap when the fence is down all around?" He did send Thomas S. Mather, Adjutant-General of Illinois, to Washington to sound out General Winfield Scott, a Virginian, on his loyalty to the new administration. Scott, who was known as "Old Fuss and Feathers," sent back these words: "Say to him that, when once here, I shall consider myself responsible for his safety. If necessary I'll plant cannon at both ends of Pennsylvania Avenue, and if any show their hands or even venture to raise a finger, I'll blow them to hell." On his journey East Lincoln was warned to keep out of the free city of Baltimore, and a plot was discovered to blow up his train. He was compelled to travel from Harrisburg to Washington in strictest secrecy, so that he literally slunk into the capital.

The farewell speech from the train platform in this final scene, like the Douglas debate speech, is a blend of several of Lincoln's utterances, starting with the moving words he actually delivered to his neighbors on this occasion. The lines about the "sentiment in the Declaration of Independence," were from his speech in Independence Hall, in Philadelphia, on Washington's Birthday, eleven days later. The mystic lines about the Eastern monarch and his wise men were from the address given to farmers in Milwaukee a year and a half previously.

There is, in this farewell speech, one group of words which seems to me a particularly fine example of Lincoln's poetry: "not knowing when or whether ever I may return." That strange and beautiful construction is comparable to "The world will little note nor long remember . . ." in the Gettysburg address.

The play ends with words written by Thomas Brigham Bishop (not, as many people suppose, by Julia Ward Howe): "His soul goes marching on." They referred originally to John Brown, whose body lay a-mouldering in the grave when the first regiments marched off to war in 1861; but they express now the most important of all facts about Abraham Lincoln—the fact that, by the eternal nature of the truths that he uttered, he can never die.

In these notes I have quoted many authorities on his life, and I shall now quote from an article, published in the *Locomotive Engineers Journal*, which provides stirring testimony to the extent of his influence upon men of good will the world over. It was written by the late B. Charney Vladeck shortly after he first came to this country, a Jewish refugee from oppression in Tsarist Russia. Vladeck had been a member of the Bolshevist Party, had voted at the meeting which

had elected Lenin their leader, and had served
in prison for his revolutionary activities. He then
emigrated to America, a man whose heart was
filled with bitterness—and he learned here that
those illusive words, liberty and equality, may
have profound meaning. He became a good and
useful American citizen, and in the last year of
his life was chosen leader of the coalition of liberal Republicans, Democrats and Labor Party
members of the Council of the City of New York.

"One of my first and most memorable lessons
in Americanization," he wrote, "was Lincoln's
Gettysburg address. When I read it and reread
it and learned it by heart, struck by its noble
clearness and sweeping faith in America, I felt
as if the whole past of this country had been lit
up by a row of warm and beautiful lights; as if
some unknown friend had taken me by the hand
on a dark and uncertain road, saying gently:
'Don't doubt and don't despair. This country
has a soul and a purpose and, if you so wish, you
may love it without regrets' . . .

"On the winding highway of American history I
picture Lincoln as a sad but gentle landscape,
permeated with the beauty of eternity. I ennobled
myself by trying to understand him, and I am
grateful to America for making him possible."

Here, in these glowing words from one who had
been a deeply skeptical alien, is the essence of what
we like to call "Americanization," but which is

actually just what Lincoln meant it to be: liberation. Those who study Lincoln most closely know
that he was no chauvinistic flag-waver—and may
God forgive the loud-mouthed Fourth of July
orators who wave the American flag boastfully in
his name. The reason that he lives today, and
still inspires so many men everywhere with the
will to shake off their chains and find freedom
and opportunity in the brotherhood of life, is
that he was essentially a citizen of the world. In
a letter from the White House, he wrote: "The
strongest bond of human sympathy, outside of the
family relation, should be one uniting all working
people, of all nations, and tongues, and kindreds."
He was never parochial, never nationalistic; he
was never heard to utter thanks for that provi-
dential accident of geography which gave us the
protection of the Atlantic Ocean. In his recorded
speeches and letters, from his earliest frontier
days, he spoke not as a representative of any
one community, any one faith or class, but as a
member of the whole human race. He was forever
conscious of the obligation of all Americans to
their brethren in all other lands—to "the Liberal
party throughout the world"—to make the democratic spirit live and grow.

In the speech that he gave in Independence
Hall, ten days before his first Inaugural, he said:
"I have often enquired of myself what great prin-
ciple or idea it was that kept this Confederacy so

long together. It was not the mere matter of separation of the colonies from the motherland, but that sentiment in the Declaration of Independence which gave liberty not alone to the people of this country, but hope to all the world, for all future time." And he added: "If this country can not be saved without giving up that principle, I would rather be assassinated on this spot than surrender it."

In his first Message to Congress, when he was discussing most soberly the results of the firing on Fort Sumter, he said: "This issue embraces more than the fate of these United States. It presents to the whole family of man the question whether a constitutional republic or democracy—a government of the people by the same people—can or cannot maintain its territorial integrity against its own domestic foes."

Four years later, at his second Inaugural, in the last weeks of his life, he repeated Christ's words, "Woe unto the world because of offenses! for it must needs be that offenses come; but woe to that man by whom the offense cometh!"